**The NCEA *Catholic Educational Leadership*
Monograph Series**

The Grammar of Catholic Schooling

Richard M. Jacobs, O.S.A.

National Catholic Educational Association

Published in the United States of America by

The National Catholic Educational Association
1077 30th Street, NW, Suite 100
Washington, DC 20007
Copyright 1997
ISBN 1-55833-198-0

Richard M. Jacobs, O.S.A., Editor
Lourdes Sheehan, RSM, Series Supervisor

Production by Phyllis Kokus
Design by Beatriz Ruiz

Second printing, 1998

Table of Contents

Overview
The NCEA *Catholic Educational Leadership* Monograph Series:
Reflective Guides for Catholic Educational Leaders   v

Preface   xv

Chapter 1
Nothing in school is happenstance...   1

Chapter 2
Evidence of the grammar: The effects of Catholic schooling   11

Chapter 3
The grammar of Catholic schooling: Why Catholic educational
leaders do what they do   23

Chapter 4
The grammar of Catholic schooling: What Catholic educational
leaders do   73

References   85

NCEA *Catholic Educational Leadership* Monograph Series:
The Grammar of Catholic Schooling

Editor:

Richard M. Jacobs, OSA
Villanova University

Series Supervisor:

Lourdes Sheehan, RSM
National Catholic Educational Association

Board of Advisors:

William Campbell, SM Portland, OR	Duane Schafer Spokane, WA
Joanne Cozzi, DC Biloxi, MS	Daniel Sherman Seattle, WA
Rosemary Donahue, SND Portland, ME	Sr. Joseph Spring, SCC Mendham, NJ
Lorraine Hurley Naugatuck, CT	Patricia James Sweeney, SSJ Holyoke, MA
Carol Kulpa Memphis, TN	Donald Urbancic Towson, MD
Helen Petropoulos Ste. Genevieve du Bois St. Louis, MO	Mary Leanne Welch, PBVM Birmingham, AL

Overview

The NCEA's Catholic Educational Leadership Monograph Series: Reflective Guides for Catholic Educational Leaders

The principal's importance...

Research studying the principalship reveals just how important principals are in fostering school improvement (Griffiths, 1988; Murphy, 1993: Smylie, 1992). Although the place where much of the action in schools transpires is in its classrooms (and hence, educational reformers focus largely upon what transpires in the teaching/learning context), much of the school's success seems to hinge largely upon the principal's ability to make sense of things in such a way that teachers become more effective in accomplishing in their classrooms what they are there to accomplish (Ackerman, Donaldson, & van der Bogert, 1996).

Perhaps principals figure so prominently in efforts to improve schooling because role expectations and personalities interact in a very powerful way, as Getzels and Guba (1957) argued nearly four decades ago. Or perhaps this effect is due simply to the eminence of the principal's office, given its focal prominence not only from an architectural perspective but also from a psychological perspective. While researchers suggest that principals do influence and shape life within schools in ways that no other single role, personality, or office can (Beck & Murphy, 1992), researchers are not at all unanimous about the conditions that make this so, as Foster (1980a, 1980b) astutely observes.

Whatever the actual reason may be, principals do occupy an important role, one vesting them with authority to articulate the school's fundamental purpose to a variety of constituents. In Catholic schools, principals may articulate this purpose at the opening liturgy of the school year and at the back-to-school night, pronouncing for all to hear "who we are," "what we shall be about," and, "the way we do things around here." Principals also reiterate their school's fundamental purpose while admonishing students or offering professional advice and counsel to their teachers. In the midst of a tragedy (for example, the death of a teacher, of a student's parent or pet, or as sadly is becoming all too frequent today, the violent and senseless death of a youngster), it is the principal who is expected to utter words of consolation on behalf of the entire school community. In these and many other situations, the principal's words can give deeper meaning to actions and events in terms of the school's purpose.

When principals effectively marshal the resources of their role, personalities, and office in leading others to share the school's purpose, teachers and students, for example, can direct their efforts toward achieving the school's goals. It is this synergy of efforts, Vaill (1986) argues, that sets "high performing systems" apart from mediocre or even good organizations. "Purposing," as Vaill describes this synergy, is that stream of leadership activities which induce in the organization's membership clarity and consensus about the organization's fundamental beliefs, goals, and aspirations (p. 91).

Without doubt, there are many Catholic school principals who capably articulate their school's purpose. In addition, these principals deftly manage what it means to be a member of the school community. In sum, these principals make it possible for others to identify their self-interest with the school's purpose.

A threat to the school's Catholic identity...

For well over a century, religious women and men and priests have engaged in *Catholic* educational purposing, making it possible for generations of teachers and students to contribute to and experience great satisfaction and outstanding achievement as they have directed their efforts to fulfilling their school's Catholic purpose. For many teachers and students, the devotion of the religious sisters and brothers and priests inspired them to such an extent that the Catholic school's identity became identified with the selfless devotion of these men and women (Jacobs, 1997b). And, rightly so.

However, in the decades following the close of the Second Vatican Council, the number of religious sisters and brothers and priests steadily declined. Meanwhile, the percentage of lay men and women who have committed themselves to the Church's educational apostolate increased markedly, although the total pool of Catholic schools (and hence, of teachers and principals) declined overall. While these trends indicate that some laity are generously responding to God's call to serve as educators in Catholic schools, as with all changes, new threats and opportunities emerge.

The exodus of religious sisters and brothers and priests from Catholic schools, however, is not the most significant issue that must be reckoned with. The paramount issue posed by this exodus concerns how the laity will receive the formation they need in order to preserve and advance the identity of the Catholic school. If lay principals are to lead their school communities to engage in *Catholic* educational purposing, they will need the philosophical, theological, and historical training that was part-and-parcel of the formation program for religious sisters and brothers and priests whose communities staffed Catholic schools. The formation that young religious received in prior generations, for better or worse, provided an introduction to the purpose of Catholic education, one that was intended to guide their decision-making once they would begin teaching and administering in Catholic schools. Without such a formative program, it is difficult to envision how, even the with the best of intentions, lay principals will engage in authentic Catholic educational purposing and foster their school's Catholic identity.

How, then, will the laity receive the formative training they need to teach and administer effectively in Catholic schools?

In fact, teacher and administrator training can be undertaken at any college or university that sponsors these programs. Typical training includes an array of courses, field experiences, and internships designed to influence how an educator will deal with the problems of practice. In most places, teacher training commences during the undergraduate years when students select education as their major. On the other hand, administrator training programs begin at the graduate level, and most programs presuppose that the aspiring administrator has attained a sufficient teaching experience to be able to develop a richer and more complex understanding about what school administration really entails. Overall, the intention behind all professional training, whether it be for teachers or administrators, is to ensure that graduates possess the fundamental skills and knowledge that will enable them to practice their craft competently.

Competence, however, is only a first step. There are other important matters that educators must address as part of their work in schools, not the least of which is the substantive purpose for which we educate youth.

Aware of this need, administrator preparation is changing (Murphy, 1992; Prestine & Thurston, 1994). Many programs now introduce students to the notion of educational "purposing," as Vaill (1986) describes it, seeking to foster in students a consciousness that the principal's purpose in schools embraces "focusing upon a core mission," "formulating a consensus," and "collaborating in a shared vision." But, it must be remembered, purposing is not cheerleading. Instead, purposing necessitates translating a vision about substantive purposes into concrete activities.

How will Catholic principals receive the training that will qualify them to translate the "grammar of Catholic schooling" (Jacobs, 1995a) into actions that symbolize the abstract values embedded in the Catholic school's purpose?

The principal and Catholic educational purposing...

To bring the moral and intellectual purpose of Catholic schools to fruition, Catholic schools need principals who can lead their faculty and students to embrace and to be animated by the Catholic vision of life. This requirement presupposes, however, that Catholic principals have received training in the philosophical and theological purposes at the heart of the Catholic educational apostolate.

Honed through centuries of the Church's experience, some of these philosophical and theological purposes challenge current practice, requiring educators to consider why they do what they do in their classrooms and schools. Other Catholic educational purposes flatly contradict current notions about teaching and administering schools. If Catholic educational leaders are to provide leadership in the Catholic schools entrusted to their ministry, they need to know and understand why and how Catholic educational philosophy and theology stand critical of some current educational trends while being supportive of others.

In addition to the theological and philosophical purposes at the heart of the Catholic educational apostolate, principals of Catholic schools also need to be conversant with Catholic educational history, particularly as this drama has been enacted in the United States. The U.S. Catholic community's epic struggle to provide for the moral and intellectual formation of its students offers Catholic principals today instructive lessons about the culture and identity of the Catholic school, its purpose and importance, as well as what educators in Catholic schools ought to be doing for students. Conversancy with the experience of the U.S. Catholic community in its attempt to educate youth will enable Catholic school principals to place the issues confronting them within a larger historical context, to see how many of the issues facing them today have been dealt with in previous generations, and to respond to these issues in concert with the lessons that can be learned from Catholic educational history.

Earlier this century, when religious sisters and brothers and priests predominated the landscape of Catholic schooling, parents could assume with relative certainty that the school's principal, at least, was familiar with Catholic educational theology, philosophy, and history. In most cases, principals were familiar with these matters and provided educational leadership steeped in Catholic educational principles. Most significantly, their training provided them a background in the purposes underlying Catholic education and, as a consequence, enabled them to speak authoritatively about the school, its programs, and its effects upon students. Ironically, it was during this era that, while most knew what the Catholic school stood *for*, few worried about how it was managed. In striking contrast, as the public today worries more and more about managing schools and links this concept to quality education, the focus upon educational purposes becomes less important and quality schooling erodes. The evidence is clear: when the principal and faculty communicate and enact a compelling vision of schooling that coincides with parental interests, students benefit from the school's program (Bryk, Lee, & Holland, 1993; Coleman, Hoffer, & Kilgore, 1982; Coleman & Hoffer, 1987).

The threat posed by the loss of the religious sisters and brothers and priests who staffed Catholic schools during previous generations is something that can be dealt with. To meet the challenge, those charged with educational leadership within the U.S. Catholic community must provide formative training for aspiring and practicing Catholic school principals. They must be prepared to communicate the nature and purpose of Catholic education and to lead others to reflect upon the fundamental purposes that give life to and guide the Catholic educational apostolate.

The evolution of the NCEA's *Catholic Educational Leadership* Monograph Series...

The NCEA's *Catholic Educational Leadership* monograph series has evolved from an extended conversation about this issue. Not only are the number of religious sisters and brothers and priests in schools declining, the number of religious vocations is also declining. Rather than bemoan this trend, the Catholic community must look forward and prepare for a future that will be characterized by increased lay responsibility for many of the Church's temporal activities. Without doubt, if Catholic schools are to survive, the laity will have to respond to God's call and bear the responsibility for providing for the moral and intellectual formation of youth. In order to fulfill their call and its concomitant responsibilities, these men and women will need specialized formation to build upon the legacy bequeathed by their forebears.

Nationally, there have been many efforts to provide this type of formative training. The United States Catholic Conference has published a three-volume preparation program for future and neophyte principals, *Formation and Development for Catholic School Leaders*. Villanova University has sponsored the national satellite teleconference series, *Renewing the Heritage*, which brought together aspiring and practicing Catholic educational leaders with recognized experts from Catholic higher education. Several Catholic colleges and universities have programs specially designed to train Catholic educational leaders. The University of San Francisco's Institute for Catholic Educational Leadership stands as a prominent example of how Catholic higher education has worked to provide aspiring Catholic educational leaders the formation they need to lead Catholic schools. At the University of Notre Dame, the Alliance for Catholic Education has prepared young Catholic adults to teach in dioceses experiencing a shortage of qualified

Catholic educators. Maybe, in the long run, the Alliance will provide a new stream of vocations to the Catholic educational apostolate and perhaps some Alliance graduates will become the next generation's Catholic educational leaders.

But, for the present, a challenge remains. Those who are called to serve as Catholic school principals deserve as much formative training as it is possible to provide them without duplicating already existing institutional efforts and depleting limited resources even further.

Whom these monographs are intended for...

The NCEA's *Catholic Educational Leadership* monograph series is designed to supplement and extend currently existing efforts by providing access to literature integrating Catholic educational philosophy, theology, and history with the best available educational leadership theory and practice. Intended primarily for aspiring and practicing principals, the monograph series is also directed at other Catholic educational leaders: graduate students in Catholic educational leadership programs, superintendents, pastors, and Catholic educators and parents, as well as members of Catholic school boards.

For principals, the monographs provide insight into the nature of educational purposing, albeit from a distinctively Catholic perspective. The variety of topics covered in the monograph series will present a wide breadth of ideas and practices conveying how principals might lead their schools to enhance their Catholic identity.

For graduate students in Catholic educational leadership programs and aspiring principals in diocesan-sponsored training programs, the monographs provide a compendium of philosophical, theological, and historical research describing the nature of educational leadership, again from a distinctively Catholic perspective. The bibliography provided in each monograph identifies where graduate students and participants in diocesan-sponsored training programs may find primary sources in order that they may put this valuable literature to practical use.

If the Catholic community is to provide formative training for educators in its schools, it is most likely that success will hinge largely upon the efforts of diocesan superintendents. As the chief educational officer of a diocese, each superintendent bears responsibility for the professional development of teachers and administrators staffing diocesan schools. The superintendent also bears responsibility for their formative development as Catholic educators. Diocesan superintendents will find in the *Catholic Educational Leadership* monograph series an expansive array of ideas and topics that will not only challenge them to reflect upon how they exercise their leadership role but also how they might exercise that role by providing formative training for educators in diocesan schools.

Some pastors, particularly those who were ordained after the close of the Second Vatican Council, have not been exposed to Catholic educational thought and may feel uncomfortable, if not reluctant, to approach their congregations about educational issues. It must be asked: What could be of more importance to a pastor than the future of his congregation, that is, the children and young men and women who will grow into Catholic adulthood at the dawn of the new millennium? In these monographs, pastors will discover provocative ideas intended to foster reflection upon how they might fulfill their pastoral responsibility to preach to their congregations about significant educational matters, whether or not their parish sponsors a Catholic school.

Finally, the NCEA's *Catholic Educational Leadership* monograph series endeavors to provide Catholic educators, parents, and members of Catholic school boards topical guides to stimulate reflection upon and discussion about the important educational responsibilities they bear. After having studied the materials contained in these monographs, it is hoped that these individuals will be enabled to make better informed decisions about what they ought to do on behalf of the young men and women God has entrusted to them. All too often, these important parental, Church, and civic responsibilities are relegated to public officials and faceless bureaucrats who have little or no acquaintance with or interest in enacting Catholic educational thought for the benefit of youth.

Inter-Institutional collaboration on behalf of Catholic Education...

Through the collaborative efforts of the Department of Education and Human Services at Villanova University and the NCEA's Chief Administrators of Catholic Education Department (CACE), outstanding Catholic educational theorists have been joined together in a long range project to provide Catholic educational leaders literature to spur their formation.

As series editor, Fr. Richard Jacobs, O.S.A., of Villanova University, has recruited outstanding Catholic educators to develop reflective guides that will enable principals to learn and to think about their important role in fostering school improvement, with a particular focus on their school's Catholic identity. His experience, both as a teacher and administrator in Catholic middle and secondary schools as well as his work in Catholic higher education and as a consultant to Catholic dioceses and schools nationwide, has provided Fr. Jacobs the background to understand the formative needs of Catholic educational leaders and to translate those needs into successful programs. As guest editor of the *Journal of Management Systems*, Fr. Jacobs has also amassed broad experience in shepherding texts from inception through publication.

Sr. Lourdes Sheehan, R.S.M., CACE Executive Director, is responsible for series supervision. In this role, Sr. Lourdes works with Fr. Jacobs to oversee the development of each monograph, ensuring that these publications are not only theoretically beneficial but also of practical significance for aspiring and practicing Catholic educational leaders. As a nationally recognized expert in Catholic education, Sr. Lourdes possesses the local and national perspective to oversee the development of a monograph series that will not duplicate but will enhance the projects and programs already functioning to form a new generation of Catholic educational leaders.

Assisting Fr. Jacobs and Sr. Lourdes are CACE representatives. These individuals have been selected to review each manuscript once it has been developed. The critical feedback offered by the CACE representatives helps Fr. Jacobs and Sr. Lourdes to work with the authors in order to ensure that the interests of each target audience will be met.

This inter-institutional collaborative effort on behalf of Catholic education is an important step forward. Bringing together representatives from Catholic higher education, a national Catholic educational organization, and seasoned Catholic educational leaders to develop a monograph series for aspiring and practicing Catholic educational leaders portends a good future. By sharing their different gifts on behalf of Catholic education, the Body of Christ will be enriched as Catholic educational thought is renewed in the formation of the next generation of Catholic educational leaders.

Using the monographs...

The volumes included in the NCEA's *Catholic Educational Leadership* monograph series are not intended to be scholarly reflections about the nature and purpose of Catholic educational leadership. While the monographs will include some scholarly reflections, they will also provide aspiring and practicing Catholic school principals practical guidance about how they might lead the men and women in their schools to engage in Catholic educational purposing.

Each monograph is written in a style that includes practical applications within the text. Each monograph is also formatted to provide reflective questions and activities along the expanded outside margins. These questions and activities have been included to help readers focus, in very practical ways, upon the important ideas and concepts being discussed. Readers are urged to take notes and to write down their thoughts and ideas as they read each monograph. Then, readers can return to their jottings and use them as they think about and plan to exercise Catholic educational leadership in the schools entrusted to them.

Were readers to complete and reflect upon the questions and activities included in the margins and to engage in the practical activities included in these monographs, readers of the NCEA's *Catholic Educational Leadership* monograph series would be better prepared to engage in Catholic educational purposing. They would not only have a more comprehensive understanding about the nature of Catholic educational leadership. They would also possess action plans for translating Catholic philosophical, theological, and historical ideals into actual practice in their schools. The ideas in each monograph, then, are not dogmatic pronouncements mandating what Catholic educational leaders are supposed to do. Rather, these philosophical, theological, and historical concepts are intended to stimulate reflective thought about what Catholic educational leadership involves and the principles upon which Catholic educational leadership might be exercised.

While the decline of religious sisters and brothers and priests in schools can be viewed as a threat to the future of Catholic education, the interest expressed by many lay men and women to follow in the footsteps of their forebears presents a tremendous resource and opportunity for the Catholic community. As the identity of the Catholic school is equated more with educational purposing than the fact of whether or not school's principal and teachers are religious sisters and brothers or priests, Catholic educational leaders can take advantage of the opportunity to form the new generation of Catholic educational leaders. These devoted men and women will carry forward the purpose of Catholic education into the 21st century, just as their forebears did at the turn of the 20th century.

On the Solemnity of the Assumption August 15, 1997

Richard Jacobs, O.S.A.
Villanova University

Lourdes Sheehan, R.S.M.
National Catholic
Educational Association

Preface

Introduction...

More than three decades after Vatican II, many aspects of parish life in the United States have undergone rather radical transformations. Perhaps the most obvious change, especially for American Catholics over the age of 40, is that the mass is conducted in English, not Latin. Or maybe, whereas prior to Vatican II some parishes boasted two (and sometime three) resident priests, three decades later, women religious and lay administrators serve in parishes having no resident pastor. Noticeably absent, too, are the legions of sisters and brothers and priests bedecked in their otherworldly garb. And, lay ministers provide many of the pastoral services parishioners formerly expected of the ordained clergy.

One aspect of parish life hasn't changed all that much, however. Whenever a bishop admonishes his pastors about contributing to the support of the diocesan high schools or vocal parents confront their pastors about the need to build or expand the parochial school, heated debate is sure to follow. Even in the post-Vatican II parish, arguments about educating youth continue to turn on the purpose of a parish and how to best utilize its financial resources—topics dominating discussion since at least the 1820s.

When it comes to sponsoring Catholic schools, the vocal majority of U.S. Catholics continues to argue, almost as vociferously as did the minority of Americanists in the 1880s, that Catholic schools unduly deplete the parish's financial resources—if only for the reason that Catholic schools serve a tiny minority of Catholic youth. (On this point, the majority is correct: one—perhaps two—of every ten Catholic youth attend Catholic school for a period of time.) More importantly, the majority continues to believe that Catholic schools engender parochial and defensive attitudes toward the nation's larger social and political context. (On this point, the opponents are erroneous: research provides evidence to the contrary.) Opponents also assert that the academic programs found in most Catholic schools are limited, especially when compared to the cafeteria of scintillating choices available to students in some public schools. (Here, the opponents state the obvious. But, one must ask—Are these non-essentials worth the cost to the taxpayers? Remember: There is no such thing as a *free* public education.)

Three decades following Vatican II, a powerful minority within Catholic parishes remains convinced, as was the majority of bishops at the Third Baltimore Council in 1884, that despite all of the shortcomings associated with Catholic schools, they continue to be the only answer because only Catholic schools provide youth the most appropriate educational program they need and deserve. The proponents continue to argue that, if only parishioners would increase their contribution to the weekly collection and pastors and bishops, in turn, would reiterate why parents should send their children to Catholic schools, more Catholic youth would be attending Catholic schools. (The proponents may be correct: research indicates that suburban Catholics generally do want Catholic schools for their children.) Proponents, now armed with other research findings gathered in the 1970s and 80s, debunk the fallacies propounded by caricatures of pre-Vatican II Catholic schools emphasizing their regimented conformity and allegedly harsh brutality. (The proponents are accurate: a value-based communitarian ethos—Christian personalism—characterizes post-Vatican II Catholic schools.) Possessing a high degree of certitude that Catholic school students are not ill-served academically, the proponents assert (again, rightly) that Catholic schools provide something no public school can—a moral formation. (Remember: most state constitutions require the state to provide all youth a free and *appropriate* education. So, the question Catholic educational leaders must answer is—What constitutes an appropriate education?)

The purpose in writing this monograph is neither to revisit this contentious debate nor tally the points scored by each side. Rather, this monograph is written in order to examine Catholic educational philosophy, history, and theology in order to isolate those principles the U.S. Catholic community believes to constitute the most appropriate educational program for youth. By isolating these principles and engaging readers in thinking about them, this monograph also endeavors to equip readers with a comprehensive rationale that will enable them to promote these principles, to engage their co-religionists and fellow citizens in meaningful discourse about the educational programs youth deserve, and to devote themselves to providing today's young Catholics the educational program they will need to take their place as the nation's Catholic leaders in the 21st century.

Perhaps at the beginning of this exercise some readers may think it foolish (if not an outright waste of time) to take a backwards glance into the heritage of the U.S. Catholic community to understand what parents and Catholic parishes ought to be providing young Catholics today so that they will be able to accept adult responsibilities in the largely mysterious world looming just beyond the horizon in the 21st century. Without doubt, Catholics in the 1890s thought precisely the same way, as they struggled to figure out just what they needed to do if they were to provide their children the most appropriate educational program they would need to function effectively as Catholic adults in the 20th century.

For the Catholic community, one whose ecclesiological self-understanding is rooted in Scripture and Tradition, the exercise of taking a backwards glance is an excellent idea. This glance not only affords the U.S. Catholic community an opportunity to take pause, to carefully reconsider complex ideas and events, and to gain insight into the history and challenges the Catholic community has confronted when raising similar questions in previous generations. Assisted by Scripture and Tradition, the U.S. Catholic community can also assess the resolutions its forebears put forward and to evaluate which of their plans worked and which didn't.

Overview of the contents...

In the monograph's first section, I will lay the groundwork for all that follows by introducing and developing the idea of a grammar of Catholic schooling. In this section, I argue that this grammar represents an educational heritage which has evolved through the generations as local Catholic communities applied Scripture and Church teaching to their unique context. In this section, I expand beyond Tyack and Tobin's (1994) seminal insight concerning the existence of a grammar of schooling, while correcting for their misuse of terms. (I believe Tyack and Tobin confuse matters a bit, identifying the syntax of public schooling rather than its grammar.) Thus, as I develop the notion of a grammar of Catholic schooling, I carefully distinguish between its grammar (i.e., the principles guiding Catholic schooling) and its syntax (i.e., the application of the rules in diverse educational contexts). Throughout this monograph, I will focus upon the former rather than the latter—and leave it to Catholic educational leaders to exercise their creativity in specifying the latter.

Knowing and understanding the difference between grammar and syntax is crucial, for this difference frames the context through which readers will conceive the set of six fundamental principles the U.S. Catholic community has used throughout the generations to define what it believes is the most appropriate educational program for youth. While some scholars dichotomize the U.S. Catholic Church into two distinct eras, the pre- and post- Vatican II Church, the existence of a grammar of Catholic schooling suggests that the substantive basis of U.S. Catholic schooling—its grammar—hasn't changed all that much over the generations, even in the post-Vatican II era.

The overriding question, then, is—What principles have guided U.S. Catholic educational leaders over the generations?

Before answering this question, I will respond in the monograph's second section to another question, the question concerning the usefulness of studying grammar. People oftentimes ask—Of what use is it? From my perspective, Newman (1927) responded best to this question, arguing that the study of grammar is useful because it inculcates those intellectual habits that make students useful not only to themselves, but also to their society and to their religion as well. What more could parents—or for that matter, the civic community—expect from its schools?

Utilizing Newman's insight, it is useful to study the grammar of Catholic for three reasons and not simply because it provides intellectual exercise (though that in itself is useful). First: Studying the grammar of Catholic schooling is useful because this increases the probability that the educational judgments made by members of the U.S. Catholic community will be informed by principles that have withstood the test of critical scrutiny over many generations. Second (and more importantly): Studying the grammar of Catholic schooling is useful for Catholics who exercise educational leadership. These individuals need to know how they might enable youth to become useful to themselves, the society, and the Church. Third: Studying the grammar of Catholic schooling is useful because it renews in this generation the set of enduring principles that make it possible to clarify "Catholic school identity," that animating core of the entire Catholic schooling enterprise.

Thus, the study of the grammar of Catholic schooling is useful for anyone who exercises Catholic educational leadership. To be effective, these women and men need a refined capability to apply the grammar and its principles to the educational context in which they find themselves. Because the study of grammar will heighten their aesthetic capabilities, those who know, understand, and apply its rules are much more apt to make competent judgments about what truly is and is not Catholic about an educational program than if they had little or no familiarity with this grammar. Through their study of this grammar, these leaders will also develop a language and conceptual system making it possible for them to promote what the Catholic community believes is in the best educational interests of youth.

Having discussed grammar's utility, I will then respond in the monograph's third section to the important question advanced earlier, namely—What rules constitute the grammar of Catholic schooling? In this section, I offer six rules. These include:

God is the beginning and end of human existence.
Education is essentially a moral endeavor.
Parents are the primary educators of their children.
The subject of education is the student.
Teaching is an intimate communication between souls.
The best educational decisions are made locally.

Since, as Newman (1927) asserts, grammar defines the normative standards that make it possible for women and men to make principled judgments about the quality of the language being used, I contrast each of the six ideals enshrined in this grammar with ideas advanced during the past two decades in debate concerning the reform of American public schooling. I elucidate these sharp contrasts neither to denigrate nor to belittle public schooling. After all, nearly 8 of every 10 Catholic youth are enrolled in the nation's public schools—and it would be ludicrous for Catholics to want anything other than a vibrant public school system for all youth, especially the nearly 25 million Catholic children enrolled in public schools. Rather, I illuminate in very specific terms the radically different vision of education that the grammar of Catholic schooling proposes for the nation's youth than that prescribed by the grammar of American public schooling.

In the monograph's closing section, I will detail some challenges the grammar of Catholic schooling implies for Catholic educational leaders, that is, parents, bishops, diocesan superintendents and vicars for education, pastors and educators in Catholic schools, and students as well. Utilizing the insights into nature of leadership provided by administrative science theory, particularly the thought emerging from the writings of Barnard (1937/1958), Selznick (1956), and Vaill (1986), I argue that the grammar of Catholic schooling offers U.S. Catholic educational leaders a lucid and convincing purpose that will motivate them to see to it that youth receive the most appropriate educational experience available. Furthermore, armed with the disciplines afforded through a careful study of the grammar of Catholic schooling, these leaders will be alert to and more capable of focusing upon and confronting the many unprincipled educational ideologies permeating contemporary educational discourse. Finally, these educational leaders will be in a better position to insure that educational programs in the nation's Catholic schools are conversant with the wisdom enshrined in the grammar of Catholic schooling.

Without doubt, Catholic educational leaders (like all educational leaders) want to improve and perfect educational programs for the benefit of youth. For Catholic educational leaders, the first step in this direction requires knowing, understanding, and being capable of applying the grammar of Catholic schooling to the educational realities confronting them. But, as *Catholic* educational leaders, this grammar also reminds these women and men that they do not have to invent an educational purpose nor do they have to mime other grammatical systems, some of which stand in stark opposition to the grammar of Catholic schooling. Because the application of Scripture and Tradition to the important educational questions raised in previous generations is readily available to the U.S. Catholic community today, Catholic educational leaders can make the collective wisdom of Catholic educational philosophy, history, and theology the animating core of the educational programs they offer youth today. These are the programs that will best prepare youth to assume their positions as the nation's Catholic intellectual and moral leaders following the dawn of the third Christian millennium.

Whom this monograph is written for...

I have written this monograph for all who exercise Catholic educational leadership. As I have asserted earlier, in the broadest sense Catholic educational leadership is a term that includes all women and men who share in the Church's responsibility to see to it that Catholic youth are provided the most appropriate educational program possible.

I hope that parents, as Catholic educational leaders, will find this monograph helpful in stimulating their reflections, particularly about their divine obligation to provide for the educational needs of their children. Indeed, the judgments Catholic parents make today about what educational program their children will receive are momentous, for these judgments not only will affect their children, but also their children's children and civil and religious society as well.

I also hope the U.S. Catholic hierarchy and its pastors, as Catholic educational leaders, will find in this monograph a convincing rationale that engenders in them the courage and conviction they will need to proclaim boldly how important the grammar of Catholic schooling is for youth. In a secularized society where the ideals and virtues that bind civil communities together are trivialized, the bishop's role as prophet requires that he needs more than ever to communicate clearly and convincingly not only what God asks of His People but also to challenge them to respond wholeheartedly to God's call. It is my hope that pastors, as the bishops' local representatives, will discover in this monograph a conceptual framework that makes it possible for them to muster the courage they need to broach the difficult and oftentimes hotly contested issues concerning how the parish community will assist its parents to provide the most appropriate education for their children. As bishops and pastors carefully study the contents of this monograph, they will soon realize that it is in the Church's very best interest to support those parents who ask their bishops and pastors for assistance in providing their children the most appropriate educational program possible.

Once, after I had completed an in-service presentation at a local Catholic school and was bounding out the front door to my car, a dedicated lay teacher followed after me. She took me aside, looked me square in the eyes, and said, "Father, I want to thank you for saying what you said today. I was renewed and am enthusiastic about what God has asked me to do. It's the first time someone has said out loud what has resounded in the silence of my heart for many years." Unfortunately, it is all too frequently that those who govern, administer, and teach in Catholic schools discover themselves caught up in the press of the day-in and day-out "administrivia" and "busyness" that are part-and-parcel of educating youth in any school. Oftentimes, these matters consume so much of an educator's day, week, month, year, and career, that it is difficult (if not impossible) to reflect on the purpose underlying why one is an educator in a Catholic school.

For my part, I hope the ideals enshrined in the grammar of Catholic schooling rekindle the fervor of the Holy Spirit in the hearts of those who minister in Catholic schools—a grace God poured out in abundance when He first called these women and men to dedicate their lives to educating His children. Assisted by this grace and equipped with the disciplines inculcated by studying the grammar of Catholic schooling, educators in Catholic schools will be able to provide the necessary leadership that will make every aspect of their school *Catholic* not only in idea but also in fact.

Lastly, I wrote this monograph for students, in general, and students in Catholic schools, in particular. Perhaps I am an idealist—hoping that the contents of this monograph will encourage these young women and men to better understand and exercise their leadership role first, by seeking and, then, by immersing themselves without hesitation in their educational program. Education, after all, exists for students and an educational program informed by the grammar of Catholic schooling will inculcate in them the knowledge, skills, and values they will need to live virtuously and to fulfill their responsibilities as adult citizens.

The consequences of any failure of educational leadership on the part of students is tragic, for when youth possess neither a purpose nor principles to guide their educational decision-making, they end up wandering aimlessly through and, in all too many cases, tragically out of school. Ultimately, these students have failed themselves and will find it very difficult, when they become adults and accept adult responsibilities, to reclaim what was so freely given during one's youth. I hope this monograph communicates the collective wisdom of the Catholic community so that the young women and men will accept and exercise their responsibility as Catholic educational leaders.

Perhaps more to the point, the contents of this monograph will provide Catholic youth a compelling purpose to engage their time, feeling, and focus in a rigorous yet comprehensive program of moral and intellectual formation. Undoubtedly, this educational program is more difficult and places more demanding expectations upon students. And yet, the consequences of any failure on the part of young Catholics to participate in this more rigorous program would be especially problematic, not only for youth themselves, but for the Church and society as well. I hope, again albeit idealistically, that young women and men will take these principles to heart, to see what the Catholic community so generously offers them, and to make the grammar of Catholic schooling the animating purpose of their years in school. The disciplines this grammar will inculcate in youth today will provide their parents, their Church, and the civic community a well-founded hope that their lives in the 21st century will be better—because of the Catholic educational leadership each of them exercised during their years in school.

I wrote this monograph for all of these educational leaders—

parents, bishops and pastors, educators in Catholic schools, and students—in the hope that my reflections about the grammar of Catholic schooling will provoke and stimulate all of these people to think about why they do what they do. To the degree my endeavor is successful, this monograph will have provided a contrast to those simplistic recipes emanating from educational reformers who zealously desire to make schools work. Unfortunately, their "quick fix" solutions fail to deal with the substantive heart and soul of education. These are the matters communicated simply, eloquently, and most compellingly in the grammar of Catholic schooling.

Chapter 1

Nothing in school is happenstance...

The notion of a "grammar" of schooling...

Two historians of American public schooling have asserted the existence of a basic "grammar" of public schooling, a grammar that is implicit in the institution of public schooling. This grammar not only impacts how public officials, parents, educators, and students think about public schooling, but more significantly, this grammar also governs how these individuals evaluate public school effectiveness (Tyack & Tobin, 1994).

Like the grammar of any language system, the grammar of American public schooling consists of rules that organize and make the institution understandable. And, just as the rules of grammar recede into the background as, for instance, when students learn how to master the intricacies of grammar and to express themselves in good speech, so too, "much of the grammar of schooling has become so well established that it is typically taken for granted as just the way schools are" (Tyack & Tobin, p. 454). Thus, while the grammar of public schooling operates invisibly behind and is veiled by the visible structures of public schooling, this grammar provides the cognitive framework making it possible for people holding very different educational ideals to judge whether or not a particular public school is a *good* school.

Before moving forward into the subject of this monograph, it might do us well to pause momentarily and to give some thought to the grammar of American public schooling and its rules. By giving some specificity to this grammar, which the authors maintain exerts so much power over the lives of those governed by its rules, we might find ourselves in a better position to understand that, even if American public schooling hasn't always taken the precise form it does today, the way it is reflects persistent assumptions and beliefs about how people believe public schooling ought to be. For much of the 20th century, these assumptions and beliefs have survived and, as public schooling has reflected these assumptions and beliefs, people had little reason to question things. But, when public schooling is not consonant with the prevailing assumptions and beliefs providing its support, the cognitive dissonance engendered by the lack of congruence between what people assume and believe schooling ought to be and what it really is, causes them to raise serious questions that challenge the status quo, educationally and politically.

The Grammar of Catholic Schooling

Reflect back upon your first study of grammar:
- *How did you learn the various parts of speech?*
- *Did your class engage in diagramming sentences on the chalkboard?*
- *At the time, did you wonder about the usefulness of learning grammar?*
- *Were a student to ask you the very same questions today, how would you explain the utility of learning grammar?*

The grammar of American public schooling...

One grammatical rule Tyack and Tobin argue exerts influence over the American public schooling is the *"graded school rule."* This rule defines the organizational and instructional structure of most, if not all, American public schools.

Doesn't it seem as if six year olds have always attended first grade—where they have struggled to learn the rudiments of reading, writing, and arithmetic? Likewise, haven't 16 year olds always been enrolled in the tenth grade—taking courses in language arts, physical education, natural sciences, the social sciences, and driver's education? In reality, organizing public schools by grades is an arbitrary decision, one making it possible to sort students according to various mechanisms, the most prominent being age.

One educational outcome made possible by the graded school rule is that students advance from one grade to the next at the completion of a specified time, normally one academic year. Failure to be promoted causes problems not only for the students who fail, but serious problems for parents, school administrators, and teachers as well.

It certainly would be possible to organize public schools according to a different mechanism than the graded school rule, for example, by student achievement or subject proficiency. But, the highly charged and sometimes very emotional discussion engendered by attempts to reorganize schooling provides evidence of the power this first rule exerts in shaping how Americans think about and evaluate public schooling.

A second rule of the grammar of American public schooling is the *"self-contained classroom rule."* This rule, too, is very influential, exercising its power, for example, by shaping how people envision what public schools should look like and how they should be designed.

School architects, for example, operate under the tacit notion that schools are buildings that fulfill a specific function, namely, to provide for the educational needs of youth. First and foremost, school architects must design classrooms to fulfill a wide variety of instructional purposes. Architects also have to adapt classrooms to the average age and size of the students who are to populate them. Think about it: a science lab, for example, is designed and equipped with the materials that teachers and students need to study science. There are demonstration tables and lab tables, replete with electrical outlets, sinks with running hot and cold water, and gas jets. Complicating architectural design a bit, although the equipment used to teach junior high or middle school science resembles that used in many high schools for teaching science, much of the furniture used in junior high and middle schools must be of a smaller scale than the equipment used in a high school lab. Then, too, architects do not design science labs like band rooms. Neither does it seem ideal to design computer labs to double as art studios. Architects must take all of these factors into consideration when they design schools and classrooms. The factor guiding school design, however, is that classrooms must be self-contained.

In addition, school buildings serve many non-instructional purposes. Therefore, architects must design spaces for activities that serve and support the school's primary purpose. Whether architects design a "cathedral of culture" as many did in the early- to mid- 1900s (Cutler, 1989), or the more sanitized and factory-like edifices prevalent in the 1970s and 1980s, self-contained classrooms have predominated school architecture in both eras.

Looking back to the heady days of the 1960s, when it was quite the vogue to construct state-of-the-pedagogical-art schools sporting "classrooms without walls" and "open classrooms," the second rule of the grammar of American public schooling suggests that the very idea of a classroom without walls or an open classroom was doomed to failure from its very inception. Not that the idea was erroneous either in theory or in practice, but the idea of a classroom without walls or an open classroom violated a fundamental rule of the grammar of public schooling, just as a speaker's confusion of person and number in a formal speech violates what the audience expects to hear. The second grammatical rule compels us to inquire, "How can a '*great* room' be a '*class* room'?" For a building to be a school, many believe it must have self-contained classrooms. For without self-contained classrooms, a building might be a multi-purpose building, a sports or exhibition arena, or a storage facility, but it just isn't a school.

Tyack and Tobin's third rule of the grammar of American public schooling mandates that these graded, self-contained classrooms must be populated by girls and boys. The two historians of American public schooling have called this the "*coeducational classroom rule.*"

In light of the fact that the sexes were segregated in American public high schools in many locales at least as late as the 1930s and 40s, it is important to recall that coeducational classrooms are a relatively recent phenomenon, historically speaking. Yet, in spite of this history, the waves of resistance to the idea of single-sex schools for American youth provide an explicit reminder that the coeducational classroom rule exerts a profound influence on educational decision-making and indeed does shape how many envision the ideal classroom population. Sound absurd?

Think for a moment about how, in the early 1990s, the suggestion that some of Detroit's public schools be segregated by sex in order to provide young African-American males role-models and mentors generated so much controversy that it had to be abandoned in rather short order. The idea that co-education is best also exerts its influence in American higher education where, in recent decades most single-sex colleges have turned their backs on their single-sex heritage to embrace coeducation.

> *Examine how your school is organized:*
> - *Is the graded school rule normative?*
> - *Identify an instance when this rule made it difficult, if not impossible, to do what you believed was in the student's best interest.*
> - *Are there alternate ways to organize your school so that it might better fulfill its basic educational purpose?*

> **What do you think about coeducation?**
>
> *List some of the pros:*
> _____
> _____
> _____
>
> *List some of the cons:*
> _____
> _____
> _____

In many cases, this "strategic planned change" was merely a survival technique reacting to a marketplace where young adults and their parents place a premium on coeducation. Yet, in spite of the research, the history of success, and the need to provide a single-sex alternative for the students who would benefit from it, most single-sex colleges have realized that they must embrace coeducation as part of their mission or, sadly, be compelled to shut their doors due to a lack of sufficient enrollment. Given the grammar of public schooling, single-sex education just doesn't seem right, at any level. The idea offends our sensibilities.

This should not prove surprising, however. For decades (if not generations), graded, self-contained, coeducational classrooms have been the familiar context within which the majority of Americans have received their education in public schools. It is a pretty familiar, if not unquestioned rule shaping how things ought to be. "Coed is better than single-sex," many Americans think, despite research demonstrating, for example, that girls enrolled in single-sex schools score higher on standardized achievement exams than do their counterparts in coeducational schools (Hansen, Hansen, Walker, & Flom, 1995). Even in the face of the evidence, Norma Cantu of the U.S. Office of Civil Rights asserts, "It's not an era we're eager to return to" (quoted in Hancock & Kalb, 1996).

This portrait of classrooms is not complete, however, if we do not also include teachers.

The fourth rule of the grammar of American public schooling focuses on these individuals, in what Tyack and Tobin (1994) have identified as the "*single teacher in each classroom rule.*" In light of this rule, teachers in public schools across the nation are in classrooms not solely because they have been trained and duly certified by state accrediting agencies as qualified professionals. In actual practice, public school teachers are placed in separate classrooms and operate in relative isolation from one another if only because this is how public schooling works in actual practice (Lieberman & Miller, 1984; Lortie, 1975).

This fourth rule frames the rather familiar portrait, at least to most Americans.

For example, in the nation's public elementary schools, individual teachers frequently spend the entire day with anywhere from 25 or 35 students, covering assorted subjects and using a dizzying array of instructional techniques to communicate course content. In contrast, the nation's public high school teachers tend to be subject-area specialists. Students come into and depart from their teachers' classrooms as the periods come and go. Some periods last 45 or 55 minutes; others, for one hour and 15 minutes. In high schools with modular schedules, class periods might continue as long as three hours. But, the same rule holds: students generally interact with one teacher in one classroom for a specified period of time and then proceed to another teacher's classroom. This happens all day long. In fact, students engage in this routine day-in and day-out, week-in and week-out, year-in and year-out, for at least 12 years until they graduate.

The fourth rule of the grammar of public schooling maintains that individual teachers are found in individual classrooms for an important purpose, namely, to provide youth instruction, if only because this is the most efficient and effective way to achieve that outcome. This relatively stable structure not only serves to organize schooling, but more importantly, the presence of individual teachers in their own self-contained classrooms enables these women and men to weave the other rules of grammar into a cohesive unity. Within the confines of their own classroom, each teacher is autonomous—with little or no outside interference. The teacher is the focal individual in the classroom. And, most probably, if a teacher is not present, instruction does not proceed.

The "*compulsory attendance rule*," the fifth rule of the grammar of public schooling, defines where youngsters will attend school. It is a far-reaching rule, mandating that every child must attend school beginning at and up to an age specified by law. Typically, school authorities assign children by "attendance zone," a concept denoting the school that students live in relative proximity to, unless they are bussed to an alternate school for other, sometimes judicially imposed reasons.

One doesn't oftentimes hear about challenges to the compulsory attendance rule, although recently some parents and state legislators have been agitating to abolish attendance zones so as to give parents greater "choice" in selecting schools for their children. Likewise, doesn't it strike the public as rather odd, when concerned parents assert that the state *cannot* require youngsters to attend school and provide their children home schooling? The suspicion about parental motives engendered in the larger commonweal by home schooling is understandable, for it flies in the face of a long history that equates the promotion of the common good with universal public education, even if it requires compelling youth to attend state-approved schools.

Even with these challenges to this rule of grammar, the persuasiveness of the compulsory attendance rule continues to wield its weighty influence. Compulsory attendance rules are ingrained into the very nature of the way people think about public schooling. Most Americans simply take this fifth rule for granted.

There are some youth, however, who flagrantly disobey this rule by "cutting class" or "playing hooky." To enforce this rule, local police provide truant officers to nab these juvenile offenders. But other youth, perhaps those most troubled and at-risk, protest even more vociferously. And, despite all of the evidence indicating that the educational level attained correlates positively with income, many at-risk youth drop-out of school in a vain hope of getting on with a "real" life. "To hell with

Reflect upon teaching and learning process in your school:
- As an experiment, inquire of your teachers: Do they prefer separate classrooms?
- How are separate classrooms helpful to the teaching/learning process?
- How do separate classrooms hinder the teaching/learning process?
- Collate these data. At a faculty meeting: discuss how this rule governs the teaching/learning process and whether there might be better ways to organize the teaching/learning process.

For a moment, imagine the situation where there were no schools because all youth were schooled at home by their parents.
- Identify what you believe youngsters need and would miss with this arrangement.
- In concrete terms, what would you have to do in order to provide those needs?
- How would you get parents involved in this enterprise?
- What would this situation require of teachers?
- How would you go about recruiting, inducting, evaluating, and rehiring teachers?

the law," is their rationale. They do not associate school with their future, believing the compulsory attendance rule does not apply to them. In response, some state legislatures, like Illinois, have enacted a "no pass, no driver's license" law to motivate drop-outs to stay in school, at least to the sophomore or junior year.

In sum, this grammar has produced the relatively stable and familiar structure of American public schooling during the 20th century, the primary examples being graded schools, self-contained, coeducational classrooms taught by individual teachers, Carnegie units, and departmentalization. Were Americans to discuss schooling along the lines diverging from this grammar, few eavesdroppers to this discussion would understand that the subject was American public schooling. Maybe "alternative schooling," but certainly not American public schooling.

Figure 1.

THE GRAMMAR OF PUBLIC SCHOOLING:
*Five Resilient Rules that Shape the Reality
and are Resistant to Change*

1. ***The Graded-School Rule***:
   An arbitrary mechanism that sorts students according to various mechanisms, the most prominent being age.
2. ***The Self-Contained Classroom Rule***:
   Everything teachers and students need is provided in one room.
3. ***The Coeducational Classroom Rule***:
   The best environment for teaching and learning is a classroom populated by girls and boys.
4. ***The Single Teacher in Each Classroom Rule***:
   The best way to organize public schooling is to place teachers in separate classrooms where they can practice their craft in relative isolation from other educators.
5. ***The Compulsory Attendance Rule***:
   All children must attend school beginning at and up to an age specified by law. School authorities assign children to schools typically defined by "attendance zone."

Adapted from: Tyack, D., and Tobin, W. (1994). The "grammar" of schooling: Why has it been so hard to change? *American Educational Research Journal, 31*(3), 452-479.

But grammar is not syntax...

Tyack and Tobin are on to something, identifying the stable structure of 20th century public schooling that has been so impervious to change. However, while their notion of "grammar" is generally accurate, reflecting standard usage of the term (i.e., "a system of rules for speaking and writing a given language," McKechnie, 1983, p. 792), what Tyack and Tobin have identified as evidence of a public school grammar, identifies instead a "*syntax*" of public schooling. In its standard usage, syntax refers to that branch of grammar dealing with "the arrangement of words as elements in a sentence to show their relationship" (McKechnie, 1983, p. 1852). Grammar, a more general and abstract concept than syntax, represents the rules that govern how people speak and write a language. Syntax, a more specific and concrete concept, identifies what people may or may not do with language in a particular context.

The difference between grammar and syntax is crucial, especially when these terms are used to identify a process of schooling. The "grammar of schooling," being more general and abstract than the "syntax of schooling," represents the substantive philosophical rationale that operates transparently and behind-the-scenes of schooling. The grammar is intangible, specifying a desired state of affairs, a philosophical "what ought to be." It clarifies a framework for decision-making about what will be in schools. The "syntax of schooling," on the other hand, is more tangible. It reflects whether and to what degree that desired state of affairs specified by the grammatical rules is actually present in particular schools. It is the syntax of schooling which people use to assess whether and to what degree a school fulfills its objectives as specified by the more transparent grammar of schooling.

Where Tyack and Tobin equate the grammar of public schooling with the rules that govern schooling, it would have been better, given the tangible evidence they cite, had they identified it as the syntax of public schooling and explained how the enacted organizations called public schools reflect a particular grammar of public schooling, that is, a philosophy of education that delimits what public schools ought to look and to function like. Among others, Aronowitz and Giroux (1991) have criticized 20th century American public education from political, cultural, and social perspectives, suggesting that the syntax of schooling reflects certain hegemonic aspects of modernism that have negatively affected the meaning and dynamics of 20th century schooling, particularly as this grammar has focused almost exclusively upon pedagogical techniques and procedures to the exclusion of dialogue, process, and exchange.

Tyack and Tobin (1994) have interpreted the evidence by using political, functional, and cultural modes as a basis for asserting that the grammar of 20th century American public schooling has generally made

A school's architecture communicates values. Take a walk around your school. Examine and evaluate its architecture:
- *What would a passerby experience your school building communicating about its core values?*
- *Within your school, is there a "climate" suggested by its architecture?*
- *Is this a more institutional or home-like climate?*
- *Overall, are things locked (to be protected) or accessible (readily available and to be used as needed)?*
- *What changes might be incorporated both inside and outside your school so that it better communicates what it stands for?*

public schooling impervious to the tides of educational reform. In the most extreme case, these implicit rules have lent credibility to organizational structures associated with public schooling, whether or not the organizational structures enacted by applying these grammatical rules have actually allowed public schools to achieve their goals. The grammar manifests itself in the culture of public schools through those "stable, underlying social meanings that shape beliefs and behavior over time" (Deal & Peterson, 1990, p. 7). Because these five rules recede into the background and operate transparently only to become evident in their tangible manifestations, it is understandable that during the 20th century, the American public, in general, and business executives (Callahan, 1962), in particular, have tended to worry more about *what* public schools are or are not doing (i.e., what research calls "schooling effects") than about *why* public schools are doing or are not doing what they are supposed do.

Undoubtedly, talking around the edges of reform is much easier than engaging in substantive discourse about genuine reform. American public schooling would be better served, however, if polite discussion about reform was to concentrate upon the philosophical notions, those rules of grammar, guiding educational decision-making and made visible in the enterprise of American public schooling.

Identifying a grammar of Catholic schooling...

During the 20th century, U.S. Catholic schooling has also provided a tangible representation of an intangible grammar. Strict discipline, uniforms, a limited core curriculum, religion classes, and religious exercises are oftentimes associated in popular consciousness with Catholic schooling and, even in the decades following Vatican II, seem rather impervious to change. In many places, these factors continue to exert a powerful influence upon parents, so much so that, in numerous national surveys, parents oftentimes cite the tangible representations of Catholic schooling as the primary motivator when making a decision to send their daughters and sons to Catholic schools.

At the outset of this monograph, it is important to note that these tangible factors symbolize something more fundamental and important to Catholic schooling, namely, a particular educational philosophy that in previous generations (and in this generation as well) continues to be enacted in Catholic schools. That is, what educators in Catholic schools have done and continue to do represents practical judgments they have made about how best to apply the rules which the U.S. Catholic community has adopted and adapted to the education of youth, given their experience as Roman Catholic citizens in a pluralistic, democratic nation. The application of these rules by educators in Catholic schools throughout the past 250 years is the "syntax of U.S. Catholic schooling," especially as it has been experienced throughout the generations by the students who have been enrolled in Catholic schools.

Again, we must remember that syntax is not grammar. In much the same way that an individual can deliver a good speech crafted by someone else or an actor can recite the lines of a script written by a playwright, just because a school might exhibit strict discipline, uniforms, a limited core curriculum, religion classes, and religious exercises, this does not mean *ipso facto* that the school is a good Catholic school. (In fact, it might well be a good Lutheran or fundamentalist Christian school.) However, to be a good *Catholic* school, those charged with the authority to make decisions must not only be familiar with but also proficient in their capability to apply the grammar of Catholic schooling to the contingencies at hand.

Figure 2.

COMPARING THE GRAMMAR AND SYNTAX OF CATHOLIC SCHOOLING

The "grammar of Catholic schooling" is the substantive philosophical rationale governing how Catholic schools are organized and operate. It is the "heart" of Catholic educational leadership. This grammar is:

- a system of rules
- general and abstract
- transparent
- why people do things

The "syntax of Catholic schooling" is the application of the grammar to the reality of educating youth in Catholic schools. It is the "hand" of Catholic educational leadership. This syntax is manifest in:

- how things are arranged
- specific and concrete practices
- manifest in tangible form
- what people do

Catholic educational leaders are those women and men who focus upon the grammar (why they do what they do), endeavoring to manifest it explicitly in the syntax (what they do). This form of leadership is not reserved solely to principals, but is entrusted to all who participate in or are concerned about Catholic schooling (e.g., parents, bishops, diocesan educational officials, pastors, parish school boards, teachers, students).

In what follows, before we identify the rules associated with the grammar of Catholic schooling, we will first direct our attention to the all-too-familiar question junior high schoolers raise when they encounter their first grammar course. "Ucckkhh," they groan as they roll their eyes, "of what use is grammar?"

After responding to this blatantly utilitarian question, we will evaluate studies exploring the net positive effects of Catholic schooling, but not to rehash the already well-publicized data. Instead, we will evaluate these net positive effects to unearth evidence pointing the way to a fundamental grammar, a distinctive philosophy of Catholic education, whose rules specify an educational culture and whose effects become evident in research data. All of this, however, serves only to provide the necessary context and to set the scene for an excursus into the six rules representing the grammar of Catholic schooling. Then, by examining these six rules, we will be in a better position to contrast the grammar of Catholic schooling with the grammar of public schooling.

Finally, we will close this monograph by drawing some practical conclusions for Catholic educational leaders. We will also alert other interested parties to some of the potentially negative consequences the grammar of public schooling portends for American youth.

Chapter 2

Evidence of the grammar: The effects of Catholic schooling

During the past three decades, social scientists have used data gathered by the United States Department of Education to investigate what effects, if any, post-Vatican II Catholic schools had upon student academic achievement. Writing in the *Brookings Review*, Viteritti (1996) offered perhaps the most succinct summary of this body of research:

> Since the seminal work of the late James Coleman and his colleagues at the University of Chicago in 1982, we have known that private and parochial schools, by and large, are more educationally effective than public schools....Their most significant finding is that Catholic schools have been especially effective in educating inner-city minority populations. Many successful parochial schools have student profiles resembling those identified with failing public schools. On the whole, however, they are less racially segregated. And, on average, they operate at a cost between 50 per cent and 60 per cent of the per capita rate of a public school. (p. 12)

These are rather impressive findings, especially when one considers as a backdrop the tumultuous context of the U.S. Catholic schooling in the three decades between 1965 and 1995. Not only had sisters, priests, and brothers virtually vanished from the landscape of Catholic schooling, so also the total number of Catholic elementary and secondary schools declined 37.9% and enrollment in the nation's Catholic schools shrank by 52.7% (NCEA, 1986, 1996).

The high tide of negativity about the future of Catholic schooling slowly began to ebb in the early 1980s, as politicians directed their ire at the nation's public schools (National Commission on Excellence in Education, 1983). Armed with research findings, Catholic school proponents became more vociferous in asserting their conviction that Catholic schools were the only institution capable of providing youth the educational program they would need to seize "the Catholic moment" (Neuhaus, 1987).

While the academic achievements of Catholic schools are noteworthy, it should be recalled that the primary purpose for establishing a Catholic school is not intellectual, but moral. Thus, social scientists have also attempted to assess whether and to what degree post-Vatican II Catholic schools have been effective in shaping their students' moral perspectives.

We turn now to this body of research. Our survey will locate where the grammar of Catholic schooling is embedded in Catholic schools. Then, in the next chapter, we will identify the grammar itself.

Studies of academic outcomes...

The two most prominent research studies, Coleman, Hoffer, and Kilgore's *High School Achievement: Public, Catholic and Private Schools Compared* (Basic Books, 1982) and Coleman and Hoffer's *Public and Private High Schools: The Impact of Communities* (Basic Books, 1987) have culled from a massive body of descriptive data some rather substantial evidence sustaining the assertion that post-Vatican II Catholic schools are effective.[1]

Coleman, Hoffer, and Kilgore's *High School Achievement: Public, Catholic and Private Schools Compared* (1982) was the first major research study featuring post-Vatican II Catholic schools. The authors' analysis revealed that private schooling, in general, and Catholic schooling, in particular, is related to greater verbal and mathematics achievement scores by private school sophomores and seniors than by their counterparts in the nation's public schools. Coleman *et. al* attributed these results to the data suggesting not only that Catholic schools, in particular, provide a safer, more disciplined and more orderly environment, but also that Catholic high school students attend more school, do more homework, and generally undertake a more rigorous (though narrower) academic program than their public school peers.

What Coleman *et al.* asserted, however, was not new. In fact, their data lent additional support to Greeley and Rossi's (1966) earlier finding that private schooling, in general, and Catholic schooling, in particular, related to greater verbal and mathematics achievement scores by private school sophomores and seniors than by their counterparts in public schools.

But, one ought to wonder, "How is this outcome possible, given the disparity in resources available to Catholic educators?"

One plausible explanation argues that educators in Catholic schools possess two significant strengths. First, they have *professional credibility*. The data clearly support this notion. Despite rather meager resources, educators in the nation's Catholic schools possess the professional skills and personal wherewithal to motivate students to achieve academically. Second, these educators possess a *clear purpose*. That is, they bring something intangible to their work, something that resources alone cannot translate into student achievement. While the data do provide support for the first strength, the data do not provide support for the second strength, if only for the reason that researchers cannot measure an intangible, for example, a teacher's "sense of vocation." Researchers first have to operationalize the concept, that is, to identify

---

Reflect on your faculty.

Identify their strengths:

List their weaknesses:

Cite those factors you attribute to their success:

how it is enacted. Only then can researchers measure it.

Without doubt, these findings provided a much needed boost in morale for proponents of Catholic schooling. Many others, especially prominent members of the research community, however, remained skeptical, challenging the efficacy of *High School Achievement*.[2] In the end, the research community was more accurate in its assessment than proponents were. Although the evidence supporting the instructional effectiveness of Catholic schools was impressive, the overall advantage portrayed in *High School and Beyond* was, in actuality, somewhat smaller than Coleman *et al.* had suggested (Raudenbush & Bryk, 1986; Willms, 1984, 1985, 1987). Perhaps it was Convey (1992) who drew the most accurate conclusion warranted by the research:

> Whatever the size of the effects, the Catholic school advantage that did occur apparently primarily was due to a homogeneous and rigorous curriculum, good discipline, and a supportive school climate, which produced positive results for students of all backgrounds. (p. 18)

What remains undisputed about *High School Achievement* and is significant as we identify the grammar of Catholic schooling are the three elements of Catholic schooling effectiveness that Coleman *et al.* specified and Convey highlighted, namely, the homogeneous and rigorous curriculum, good discipline, and a supportive climate. Unfortunately, while these characteristics are important and may indeed "sell" Catholic schools to parents who are wary of a public school system reputed to lack these essential elements of good schooling (particularly in the nation's urban centers), these effects are not what makes a Catholic school distinctively *Catholic*. These quantifiable factors do provide evidence of something deeper, namely, a grammar of Catholic schooling. It is this fundamental purpose that guides the day-to-day and year-to-year educational decisions being made in Catholic schools. This purpose exerts itself and becomes evident in curriculum, discipline, and climate of Catholic schooling, functioning as an operative rationale to unify the many diverse aspects of life in Catholic schools.

Turning to the second study, published five years after *High School Achievement*, Coleman and Hoffer (1987) utilized longitudinal data and more powerful statistical tools to revisit the interactions between predictors of student achievement and type of school. Publishing the results of their research in *Public and Private High Schools: The Impact of Communities*, the authors asserted that while much of the data reconfirmed the original proposition (Coleman *et al.*, 1982), the benefit of the longitudinal data and the availability of more powerful statistical methods enabled the authors to confirm Greeley's (1982) proposition that Catholic schools do raise the academic achievement of populations that traditionally achieve at lower levels, particularly, children from

---

Conduct this Catholic school "culture building" exercise:
- *Track your students after graduation.*
- *Survey your graduates. Invite them to cite the singlemost influential experience during their years at your school.*
- *Highlight and celebrate these experiences, for example, by inviting alumni/ae to share their experiences with your current student body and incorporating these stories into your school's induction process.*

families providing lower levels of parent support and/or children from families with lower socioeconomic status, especially Blacks and Hispanics. Coleman and Hoffer (1987) gave proponents good reason to be ecstatic: the data confirmed that Catholic schools were effective, particularly in those troublesome neighborhoods where educating the nation's youth is most difficult. This time around, the response of the research community was muted, but not silent.

To identify the grammar of Catholic schooling, however, we must pay careful attention to an assertion made by the authors of *Public and Private High Schools*, namely, that Catholic schools, when compared to their private and public counterparts, exhibit the lowest dropout rate and, furthermore, their graduates who do go to college were more likely to stay in college. Evidently, something transpires within Catholic schools that either invites, challenges, or compels students to envision their future lives as being connected in some important way to what transpires in these schools. An intangible "*something*" is communicated through the process of Catholic schooling, that is, a taken-for-granted pattern of basic assumptions and values binds together the many things that are done in Catholic schools into a unified educational experience which causes students to identify themselves and their aspirations with "the way we do things around here" (Schein, 1984).

Based upon their analysis of these data, Coleman and Hoffer (1987) theorized that, because Catholic schooling takes its existence from a religious community, these schools exhibit a higher level of "social capital" when compared to other public and private schools. Functionally, the authors argued, the religious community (e.g., the parish, the sisters and brothers and priests, the connection with the diocese and its bishop as well as the Pope and the universal Church) provides a framework governing what transpires in Catholic schools. In addition, a strong academic curriculum, a controlled, communal atmosphere, as well as social resources and relationships enculturating students through the school's core technology (i.e., instruction and learning) interact powerfully to produce positive outcomes in student achievement. Evidently, these cultural forces positively impact student achievement.

Again, the three factors quantified by this research (i.e., a strong academic curriculum, a communal atmosphere, and, social resources and relationships enculturating students into the school's academic purpose) point to an intangible purpose, the grammar of Catholic schooling. *What* Catholic schools do is demonstrated in these effects. However, the purpose guiding *why* Catholic schools do these things, the rules of grammar governing Catholic schooling, lie behind and are themselves embedded in these effects. It is this grammar we need to ferret out if Catholic educational leaders are to exercise their legitimate authority and to proclaim more effectively why Catholic schools do what they do as

---

Conduct informal interviews of your faculty and students.

Identify three activities which communicate your school's purpose:
1) _____
2) _____
3) _____

Identify three activities which develop your students' social capital:
1) _____
2) _____
3) _____

Identify three educational activities you believe are essential for the survival of American Catholicism:
1) _____
2) _____
3) _____

well as how Catholic schools fulfill the common school ideal, the forgotten heart and soul of American public education.

In sum, these two post-Vatican II research studies provide ample data describing what Catholic schooling does effectively and give the American Catholic community a snapshot detailing the effects of Catholic schooling. However, as important and useful as this snapshot is for identifying with greater precision what Catholic schooling has provided its students in the decades following the Second Vatican Council, it must not be forgotten that these studies have not informed the American Catholic community just why it is that Catholic schools do what they do. In short, the quantitative approach to conducting research has generally overlooked or neglected the rich character and culture of Catholic schooling, what a portrait of Catholic schooling would convey.[3]

Just as good speech is one net positive outcome emanating from the proper application of the rules of grammar, so too, the net positive effects of Catholic schooling evidence a more substantive matter, namely, the grammar of Catholic schooling. Rather than meandering along this narrow descriptive pathway, in a vain search for data that will convince critics that a vibrant system of Catholic schools is in the nation's best interest, it would be better to examine Catholic schooling from a normative perspective, that is, to elucidate and highlight the deeper dimensions of meanings and purposes embedded in and conveyed through the snapshot of Catholic schooling effectiveness. This task requires researchers to envision *why* Catholic schools do *what* they do, to think about the textures and hues, those elements adding depth and character to a study of Catholic schooling. Only a rich portrait can communicate the essential purpose of Catholic schooling, for example, to parents who are confused about their responsibilities as the primary educators of their children, particularly in an era where skepticism about social institutions, like public schools, is rife.

In proposing a grammar of Catholic schooling, the truly remarkable outcome of the research conducted during the 1980s and 1990s is not what Catholic school proponents have seized upon, namely, that Catholic schools do what they do effectively and in a less costly manner. More importantly, the evidence reconfirms the efficacy of the basic thrust governing *why* Catholic schools do *what* they do.[4]

At the same time, however, while research examining post-Vatican II Catholic schooling substantiates the assertion that Catholic schooling provides students a fundamentally sound academic program, especially for those who come from lower-middle class and poor families, we must not forget that this utilitarian rationale is not the purpose for which the Church sponsors schools or that educators to devote their lives to Catholic schooling. Fundamental competence in school management, human relations, and educational technology serve only as a foundation upon which schools bring their purpose to fruition

Survey your faculty:
- *What concrete factors motivated them to dedicate themselves to teaching in a Catholic school?*
- *What experiences have encouraged your teachers in their ministry?*
- *In what ways might you provide your faculty the encouragement that will nourish their vocation?*

(Sergiovanni, 1995).

Further research is required if we are to identify how Catholic schools, as *Catholic*, are distinctive and whether Catholic schools are effective in fulfilling their moral purpose. How that value-added distinctiveness can be described, studied, and validated is a challenge for researchers. But, success in this endeavor will make it possible to identify truly effective Catholic schools and to offer assistance to those that aren't so that they might become effective also.

Studies of moral outcomes...

While the academic outcomes associated with post-Vatican II Catholic schooling effectiveness have received the lion's share of public notice, of far greater significance is whether and to what degree Catholic schools are effective in communicating their moral purpose.

One early study of post-Vatican II U.S. Catholic schooling indicated that by the mid-1960s Catholic education greatly resembled public education both in structure and content (Greeley & Rossi, 1966). For Catholic school proponents, this wasn't necessarily good news, if simply for the reason that the differences evidencing themselves were due primarily to parental religious belief and socioeconomic class and not to Catholic schooling. Greeley and Rossi were unequivocal (and, some have argued, incorrect) in judging the relevance of Catholic schools to the Church's future: "[T]here is no evidence that Catholic schools have been necessary for the survival of American Catholicism" (1966, pp. 227-228).

Fifteen years later, the National Opinion Research Center (NORC)—at the behest of the Knights of Columbus—conducted a second survey of student moral attitudes to determine what the case actually was (cited in Walch, 1996, p. 232). The NORC study indicated that Catholic schools indeed were effective in shaping student morals, albeit in limited rather ways. The data revealed that students who attend Catholic schools are more likely to go to Mass, to consider a religious vocation, and to oppose abortion. This was good news. In other significant ways, the news wasn't so good. The data revealed that Catholic schools were perhaps ineffective because students attending Catholic schools exhibited *no* significant difference in their attitudes toward prayer and sexual morality than did their peers who were enrolled in other schools.

The third study investigating Catholic schooling, first initiated in 1981, examined the distinctive features of effective Catholic high schools and the ways in which these factors combine to form a supportive culture that promotes academic achievement for a broad cross-section of students. The results of this analysis, published 12 years later in Bryk, Lee, and Holland's *Catholic Schools and the Common Good* (1993), weaves quantitative analyses of large national databases, qualitative portraits of seven Catholic high schools, as well as intellectual explorations of the theological, philosophical, and historical foundations of Catholic high schooling. The result of this research is an artistic and impressionistic tapestry which the authors maintain portrays U.S. Catholic high schooling in the 25 years following the close of Vatican II.

In sum, Bryk *et al.* (1993) argue that post-Vatican II Catholic high schools do have an independent effect upon student achievement, especially in reducing disparities between disadvantaged and privileged students. Catholic high schools achieve these outcomes, the researchers maintain, as a consequence of four factors: a delimited technical core; a communal organization; decentralized governance; and, an inspirational ideology.

The *delimited technical core*, the technology of Catholic schooling, is the humanistic education required of all students. Bryk *et al.* argue: "At base is an active institutional purpose, the aim of a common education of mind and spirit for all, that integrates these structures and policies" (p. 298). In Catholic high schools, what is important is not so much what courses a student takes (electives are limited in content and number), but that the same basic academic goals apply for everyone.

What may appear on the surface to be a curricular deficit may indeed be its very strength. For, as students partake of a common curriculum, they develop a shared common language, conceptual, and symbol system, what Bryk *et al.* identified as "humanistic" and Hirsch (1987) has called "cultural literacy." In short, because Catholic high schools provide a competently taught delimited technical core, students come to know and understand the language, concepts, and symbols associated with the school's Catholic identity (LaPlante, 1992). Whether or not individual students (or educators, for that matter) actually believe in and practice the elements which are part of that ethos is an entirely different matter. The important point is that the elements of Catholic culture (namely, its language, concepts, and symbols) are transmitted effectively through the school's common curriculum, delimited and technical as it is (McLaren, 1986).

The *communal organization* of Catholic schooling represents the array of activities, structural components, and shared beliefs that provide a common ground among and between school members, whether these individuals are administrators, teachers, students, or parents. The "common ground established here orders and gives meaning to much of daily life...." (Bryk *et al.*, p. 299). Because what is done in Catholic schools is done for a purpose, the school is able to sustain and enculturate a diverse body of people into a functioning educational community. And, while individual rights are respected in Catholic schools, responsibility for upholding the common good is an expectation of every member. Failure to uphold the common good carries real sanctions, both formal and informal.

> *How might the Catholic school's curriculum, oftentimes experienced as limited, actually be its strength?*

> *"Unity in purpose." "Diversity in action." Catholic schools have a common purpose and communal organization.*
>
> *How does this evidence itself in your school's:*
> - *governance?*
> - *curriculum?*
> - *instruction?*
> - *discipline?*
> - *relationships with local parishes?*

The Grammar of Catholic Schooling

> **Subsidiarity asserts that the best decision is made locally. In light of this principle:**
> - *Explore the relationship between the diocesan educational office and your school. How might diocesan officials help your school to better fulfill its Catholic purpose?*
> - *List the ways teachers are leaders in your school. What does their leadership require of you, especially if they are to be successful in transmitting your school's purpose?*
> - *Reflect upon the principal's role in a school characterized by subsidiarity. What does subsidiarity require of you (and others) if you are to encourage them to bring your school's purpose to fruition?*

While the Catholic school is organized as a community and this absolutely requires uniformity in purpose, it does not necessitate absolute conformity in function. Ideally, every member of the Catholic school community desires to belong to it and to be a valued and contributing member of it. Thus, like ancient civilizations which banished members for engaging in taboo behaviors and violating sacred mores, so too, the communal organization of Catholic schooling militates against anomalies that have the potential to threaten its unity of purpose. Interestingly, however, the number of students expelled annually from Catholic schools indicates that there is, in reality, a very spacious terrain demarcating unity of purpose and individual self-expression in Catholic schools (Yeager, Benson, Guerra, & Manno, 1986).

Catholic high schooling, the authors argue, is also characterized by *decentralized governance*. For Bryk *et al.*, decentralization—which is "predicated on the view that personal dignity and human respect are advanced when work is organized in small communities where dialogue and collegiality may flourish" (p. 302)—represents "the set of fundamental beliefs and values that constitute the spirit of Vatican II" (p. 300).

Unfortunately, this characterization is neither precise nor adequate. Catholic schooling in the United States has always been characterized by decentralization, albeit under a different rubric, that of subsidiarity. For example, pastors *not* diocesan officials have for decades possessed rather considerable latitude in making decisions about what transpires in the parochial school (Dolan, 1985). Likewise, religious sisters and brothers and priests have exercised relative independence in educational decision-making for the schools entrusted to them (Jacobs, 1997b). The relative independence of local authorities is one implication of the theory of subsidiarity, that is, the philosophical notion positing that the best organizational decisions are those made locally.

That Bryk *et al.* (1993) have discerned the continuing presence of subsidiarity operative in the schools of the post-Vatican II Church not only provides an indication of its pervasiveness, indeed, but also evidence that subsidiarity is one rule governing how Catholic schooling has been and continues to be organized.

Lastly, the authors of *Catholic Schools and the Common Good* argue that an *inspirational ideology* evidences itself in effective Catholic high schools. Steeped in Christian personalism, that is, "humaneness in the myriad of mundane social interactions that make up daily life" (Bryk *et al.*, 1993, p. 301), this inspirational ideology informs its members in such a way that *what* is done reflects something more important, namely, *why* it is done. The authors have identified three principles demarcating this inspirational ideology:
- a belief in the capacity of human reason to arrive at ethical truth;
- the affirmation of a public place for moral norms; and,
- the power of the symbolic as an integrative force in human life.

For Bryk *et al.*, the delimited technical core, communal organization, decentralized governance, and inspirational ideology identify what post-Vatican II Catholic high school effectiveness is, that is, how these four factors interact powerfully to convey an institutional purpose integrating the school's structures and policies with the people who comprise the local Catholic educational community. Again, while each of these four factors is important (for each does provide for a richer understanding about what Catholic schooling accomplishes), the delimited technical core, communal organization, decentralized governance, and inspirational ideology also provide evidence of a fundamental grammar of Catholic schooling, a series of rules that govern why Catholic high schools do what they do (and evidently do quite well). It is this grammar that needs to be explicated if the real success of Catholic schooling is to be understood and proclaimed.

As I have noted elsewhere (Jacobs, 1996), these four factors comprise the culture of the Catholic school and are the critical variables in Catholic schooling if students are to know, understand, appreciate, value, and ultimately, to make the school's Catholic identity their own. This does not mean that students who attend Catholic schools will *ipso facto* believe in and practice the Catholic religion merely as a consequence of having attended Catholic schools for eight or twelve years. What the Bryk research indicates is that educators in the Catholic schools of the 1960s, 70s, and 80s continued to provide a moral formation for their students, in particular, as these educators inculcated in their students that humanistic form of cultural literacy shared by the Catholic community (Bryk *et al.*, 1983). In a world riddled by the specter of moral relativism, skepticism, blatant and unashamed materialism, and agnosticism (if not outright atheism), these educators have preserved and communicated the school's distinctive Catholic identity. What their students will do with their moral formation, that is, how they will act on it as adults, is a task this generation must leave for future researchers to investigate.

A fourth study to ascertain the effectiveness of Catholic schools in promoting positive moral outcomes in their students was undertaken in the early 1990s by Educational Testing Service (ETS), nearly three decades after Greeley and Rossi published their research. The results of the ETS study, for the most part, substantiated the 1981 NORC findings. That is, out-of-school religious education programs appear to be almost as effective as parochial school programs in handing on the faith to the next generation (Sommerfeld, 1994).

While proponents might have been stunned by the ETS findings, the study made a helpful contribution to research about the effectiveness of the programs of moral formation found in the nation's Catholic schools. While opponents could seize upon the ETS study to indict Catholic schools and, in a reactive mode, proponents might wish to the

---

Identify three behaviors you would wish to see your graduates practice because they have attended a Catholic school:

a)_____

b)_____

c)_____

Solicit ideas from your faculty about how they might incorporate these behaviors into the school's formal and informal curriculum. How might this endeavor be assessed?

best "spin" on the results by citing the flaws inherent in the ETS study, it would be better if proponents accept the data at face value and admit that many religion programs are not nearly as effective as everyone would hope. And, proponents should be especially determined to assist each and every Catholic school to continuously improve its program of religious formation so that every student knows, understands, and experiences the faith of the Catholic community better than do those students who do not attend Catholic schools.

At the same time, it would be well if opponents of Catholic schools would remember that Catholic schools are not seminaries. Simply put: Catholic schools do not exist to indoctrinate students in the faith and practice of the Church. Rather, Catholic schools exist because parents want their daughters and sons to receive an integrated program of moral and intellectual formation that will enable them to function effectively as American Catholic adults. As this educational program specifically concerns the moral formation of youth, it is only a well-conceived, well-executed, and integrated religion program (one teaching students the faith and practice of the Church as well as providing students a supportive culture wherein they learn—as Newman (1927/1987) suggested—to think of matters as Catholics do) that will form the leaders which the Church will need in the next generation.

In the era prior to Vatican II, an era when the Church was characterized by institutional hues, inculcating the Catholic ethos in Catholic schools was known by the term "permeation theory." That is, teachers and administrators in Catholic schools were challenged to infuse the Catholic ethos into every aspect of Catholic schooling. Indeed, permeation theory was so influential by the 1950s that textbook publishers were forced to adapt standard mathematics textbooks to use Catholic religious symbols in problem-solving (e.g., by using rosary beads and statues of the Blessed Virgin in computation exercises). Textbook publishers also adapted the secular version of the basal reading series featuring Dick, Jane, and Spot to reflect Catholic themes (Luke, 1991).

Like the Church of the post-Vatican II era, permeation theory has taken on a more personalistic ethos. That is, rather than focusing on externals, permeation now challenges educators in Catholic schools to embody for their students the distinctive values at the heart of Catholic discipleship (NCEA, 1988). In the NCEA's *Visions and Values* program, for example, these values include community, faith, hope, reconciliation, courage, service, justice, and love.

Although the ETS study challenges the efficacy of religion classes, Bryk *et al.* offer hope about the witness educators in Catholic schools provide youth. Indeed, the research suggests that Catholic schools may not be exemplary in teaching religion, but they are quite effective in transmitting the Catholic ethos. The good news is that the programs of

---

Rank the overall effectiveness of these elements of your school's total educational program ("1"-most successful; "4"-least successful):

_____ *intellectual formation*
_____ *social formation*
_____ *moral formation*
_____ *religious formation*

moral formation which Catholic schools offer their students do permeate the entire curriculum as teachers bring the Catholic ethos into the concrete reality of learning in their classrooms. Much work remains, however, if Catholic schools are to be characterized as educational communities where the faith and practice of the Catholic Church permeate every classroom in every Catholic school and if Catholic schools are to be as effective in fulfilling their moral purpose in the 21st century as they have been in fulfilling their intellectual purpose during the 20th century.

The research and the grammar...

Catholic school effectiveness, whether measured in terms of outcomes on standardized achievement tests or surveys of religious and moral attitudes, is not due simply to the fact that Catholic schools provide a safer, more disciplined, and more orderly environment. Nor are Catholic schools effective simply because their students attend more school, do more homework, and generally undertake a more rigorous (though narrower) academic program than their public school peers do. If Catholic school effectiveness was due to these factors alone, replicating these factors in public schools across the nation would provide an immediate curative for all that allegedly ails American public schooling.

While many genuinely concerned citizens may be sympathetic to this line of reasoning, the conclusion is nothing but sheer nonsense. Veiled behind the effects of Catholic schooling and wielding its erstwhile influence to produce them is a grammar that provides a normative framework for decision-making in the nation's Catholic schools. What was and continues to be enacted in Catholic schools represents not a recipe for success but rather the application of a distinctive body of rules that Catholic educational communities have adopted and adapted, given their experience as Roman Catholic citizens in a pluralistic, democratic nation, to provide the best possible moral and intellectual formation program for youth.

Unfortunately, the principled decision-making process required by this distinctive grammar cannot be cloned or duplicated, especially in schools where the moral formation of students has been vitiated from the curriculum and the moral responsibilities of educators must be ignored in educational decision-making.

We turn now to the six rules of the grammar of Catholic schooling. We will first define and apply each rule to the practical realities of Catholic educational decision-making. We will then use each rule to critique educational decision-making as it has become evident in discussions and debate about reforming American public schooling.

Notes

1 Other prominent studies might have been included in this survey, however, these two studies utilize national data, present fewer methodological problems than some of the other studies, and each has been critically evaluated by those who are friends (as well as those who are foes) of private education.

2 See: Alexander, 1987; Alexander & Pallas, 1983; Goldberger & Cain, 1982; Heynes & Hilton, 1982; Keith & Page, 1985; McPartland & McDill, 1982; Murnane, 1981; Noell, 1982, 1983. Notable scholarly journals, too, such as the *Harvard Educational Review* (November, 1981) and *Sociology of Education* (April/July, 1982; October, 1983; July, 1985), jumped headfirst into the fray, devoting special issues to this debate.

3 It was Lightfoot (1983) who first explicated this essential difference by providing six portraits of good schools. What is important about Lightfoot's work is her shift from a descriptive paradigm to a normative paradigm which enabled her to move beyond quantitative research and an excessive concern with measuring attributes associated with effective schools (e.g., student scores on standardized exams, rates of acceptance into college of first choice) into the realm of qualitative research and an interest in aesthetic and moral effects associated with good schools (e.g., the development of personal character). It is the difference between Catholic schooling effectiveness and Catholic schooling goodness that the grammar of Catholic schooling illuminates.

4 Unfortunately, there is scant evidence of any significant discussion about this important matter in literature promoting Catholic schools. Instead, many of those who promote Catholic schooling tend to focus almost exclusively upon the narrow matter of schooling effects and per pupil savings to local school districts, rather than articulating the more compelling moral argument that proclaims the theological, philosophical, and historical purpose that is the heart and soul of these effects.

Chapter 3

The grammar of Catholic schooling: Why Catholic educational leaders do what they do

As rector of the newly established Catholic University of Dublin, John Henry Newman regularly gathered his faculty together and proceeded to lecture them. Oftentimes, Newman's ostensible purpose was to remind his colleagues of the nature and purpose of a Catholic university. Newman's passion for Catholic education was particularly evident in those lectures where the rector spoke to his faculty about their responsibility for bringing the university's purpose to fruition.

In one dramatic lecture, Newman invented a fiction describing the plight of one applicant to a university, one "junior Mr. Brown." Sadly, this chap failed his exam. (In reality, the entrance exam was more of an applicant's nightmare-come-true, that is, an interrogation featuring a university tutor who grilled applicants to determine their dexterity in analyzing the grammatical elements of classical literature.) The young Mr. Brown's father desperately wanted his son to be admitted to the university and, upon receiving news of his son's failure, the senior Mr. Brown expressed his disaffection by firing-off a letter to the tutor.

In this letter, the senior Mr. Brown informed the tutor that the study of grammar is concerned with trifling technicalities which, he asserted, "serve only to quench the vigor of youthful minds." In the senior Mr. Brown's estimation, the tutor should have taken much greater notice of the junior Mr. Brown's expansive wealth of knowledge about so many other things, presumably learned at an elite preparatory school.

Of the many points Newman was asserting through his fiction, one concerned the fallacy of concluding that the study of grammar is unnecessary and unimportant simply because students do not enjoy learning grammar. The senior Mr. Brown's fundamental error, in Newman's estimation, was his failure to appreciate why grammar is a curricular requirement in the first place.

Grammar is an essential component of the curriculum for the reason that its technicalities inculcate in students aesthetic judgment, that is, the ability to discriminate between *good* and *bad* language. This refined capability, when applied to other areas of human existence is, for Newman, what eventually will make students useful not only to themselves, but also, to their society and religion. Thus, for Newman, grammar is an indispensable curricular requirement, one that does not serve the utilitarian purposes held by many parents, especially those like the senior Mr. Brown. For Newman, teaching is a purposeful activity not merely providing entertainments for students.

In much the same way, this tedious process of ferreting-out and clarifying the grammar of Catholic schooling proves itself to be rather frustrating for proponents of Catholic schooling whose more pressing interests force them to seize upon slogans, public relations campaigns, and media efforts to wage their campaign on behalf of Catholic schools. Unfortunately, it is only the slow, arduous, and painstaking clarification of this grammar that ultimately will provide proponents of Catholic schooling a moral framework enabling them to make principled judgments about good and bad schooling and, by virtue of this aesthetic, to appreciate the value of Catholic schooling, to proclaim its compelling vision, and to convince their fellow citizens that a vibrant system of Catholic schools serves the nation's common good.

Figure 3 lists the six rules comprising the grammar of Catholic schooling. These rules serve as the secure foundation upon which educators in Catholic schools build their students' moral and intellectual achievements.

Figure 3.

THE GRAMMAR OF CATHOLIC SCHOOLING
*Six Rules Influencing Student
Moral and Intellectual Achievement*

At least six rules comprise the grammar of Catholic schooling. These include:
1. *God is the beginning and end of human existence.*
2. *Education is essentially a moral endeavor.*
3. *Parents are the primary educators of their children.*
4. *The subject of education is the student.*
5. *Teaching is an intimate communication between souls.*
6. *Educational decisions are best made locally.*

In this chapter, we will explicate each rule with a view toward understanding with greater clarity and precision what each rule means as well as what each implies for actual practice. Once we explicate the six rules, we will then synthesize them and, by proceeding in this way, we will be in a better position to conceptualize how the six rules interact dynamically to produce the effects noted in the descriptive research considered in the previous chapter. In addition, we will also see how these six rules provide Catholic educational leaders a substantive purpose that can guide decision-making (Vaill, 1984). This having been accomplished, the monograph's closing chapter will consider some of the many implications the grammar of Catholic schooling implies for Catholic educational leaders.

Rule #1: God is the beginning and end of human existence.

The Book of Genesis is unambiguous in its claim that there is but one God. The text further adds that God has created all things, has introduced order into the chaotic universe, and is the origin of justice. Whether a reader resonates more with the Elohist tradition, emphasizing the transcendent God who created humanity in His own image (Genesis 1:27ff), or the Yahwist tradition, emphasizing the immanent God who formed every human being out of the earth's dust and breathed into their nostrils the divine breath of life (Genesis 2:7ff), both textual traditions affirm the faith of those who taught that one God is the source and ground of human existence.

Furthermore, this biblical tradition proclaims that because human beings are God's creatures, they did not emerge through random, chance occurrence. Neither are they victims of Fortune's whims or subject to the Fate's wiles. Instead, human existence has profound meaning and value because God has breathed His divine life and purpose into every human being. For Catholic educational philosophy, it is the discovery of this purpose, the end of human existence, that is the defining activity shaping and guiding learning as well as assisting students to become responsible agents in this world, the means to their end—in God.

In the creation story, the authors also relate that God rested when He completed work on the sixth day of creation. "*Shabbat*" (or Sabbath), for faithful Jews, denotes "to rest," that is, to cease from all the work one has to do and to rest, just as God did on the seventh day (Genesis 2:2). But, when faithful Jews truly rest, *Shabbat*, they do not sleep. Rather, *Shabbat* is an active rest wherein faithful Jews dwell together in *Shalom*, a state of being in God's presence and one with Him. "*Shabbat, Shalom*" is the beautiful Jewish greeting whereby human beings remind one another of their proper beginning and end, that is, restful peace in God.

The belief that God alone is the beginning and end of human existence is the wellspring of the grammar of Catholic schooling, its primary rule. Created by God, human beings are endowed with divine purpose. Coming from God, each and every human being exists to become ever more perfectly the divine life that is the image and likeness of God has already breathed into them. Theologically, humans learn, work, pray, love, laugh, study, and die seeking in all things to become more perfectly what they truly are. And, as human beings become ever

---

Read the Creation traditions related in the Book of Genesis (1:27ff and 2:7ff):

Identify differences in the two traditions (e.g., how each tradition treats of God and God's relationship to His creation):
_____
_____
_____

Identify the similarities in each tradition:
_____
_____
_____

Identify three implications these traditions have for Catholic schooling:
1)_____
2)_____
3)_____

> - *Design a paraliturgical service that uses the creation traditions to inform students of their human dignity and the purpose of their lives.*
>
> - *Organize a faculty meeting that focuses upon how each teacher will translate the paraliturgical service into classroom activities that renew the creation traditions and reaffirm the significance of each individual as a member of the school community.*

more fully God's creatures, they also become for one another a revelation of God's life and love, a living sacrament of what all humans are called to be. The complete realization of this outcome, theologically speaking, is the Kingdom of God.

Education, in this rich theological context, is that purposeful activity which draws this innate reality out of each student's innermost depths. Through the educational process, youth are reminded of the source and purpose of their existence, the Creator, and the need to convert from concern and preoccupation with self to concern and preoccupation with living in God's presence and doing God's will.

Narrowing the concept of "education" to formal education and, in particular, to what educators do in schools, this biblical imperative implies that every educational activity discovers its authentic referent in this theological vision of the human person as God's creature. Students take courses, not merely for the knowledge, skills, and interest they convey and stimulate. But, more precisely, students take courses as a means to discover their true identity as children of God, that is, people called by name to become more God-like in and through their human existence. In schools that endeavor to inculcate this ideal, students grow as God's children.

The secular grammar of American public schooling stands in stark contrast to this theological grammar. Public schools exist to provide the nation a literate citizenry and workforce. Through its educational agencies and agents, the state provides a curriculum through which youth acquire the knowledge and skills they will need so as to take their place one day, in the not too distant future, as adult citizens and to secure full-time, sustaining employment. In public schools, extracurricular activities provide students opportunities to socialize, experience excitement and amusement, or simply to be distracted. The grammar of American public schooling also leaves no room for liturgy (unless a non-religious liturgy is envisioned, for example, a pep rally for the football or basketball team or even a moment of silence at the beginning of the day before the Pledge of Allegiance). Sadly, however, this secular grammar absents the substantive source from which human existence draws its purpose, replacing it with a utilitarian rationale for students to engage in learning activities and exercises that will lead, hopefully, to the development of healthy and productive adult citizens.

Centuries after the primeval traditions of the Judaeo-Christian heritage were first preserved in the Book of Genesis, Augustine of Hippo, a Christian convert who attended the equivalent of public elementary and secondary schools in northern Africa, began the introduction to his confession of faith: "For Thou hast made us for Thyself and our hearts are restless till they rest in Thee" (*Confessions* I.1b). Augustine had come to the realization that human beings cannot experience *Shabbat, Shalom* unless they rest in God, the beginning and end of human existence.

Nearly 1500 years later, George Johnson, the Secretary General of the National Catholic Educational Association (NCEA) seized upon this rich theological tradition in his 1942 speech to the NCEA delegates when he said:

> Now nothing degrades a human being like being cut off from the God who made him. Ignorance of things divine, obtuseness to spiritual values, absence of religion affect the fundamental human quality in people. Man is understandable only in relation to his Maker. He was made to the image and likeness of God and, unless he devotes his life to developing the divine potentialities within him, he becomes progressively lower even in human stature....All of this we Catholic educators know. Our task it is to translate our knowledge into power. (1942, pp. 67-68)

For many, the fundamental rule governing the grammar of Catholic schooling reveals nothing new, expressing well what many people know intuitively, namely, that when the proper end of schooling is effectively voided from schooling, the means of education become the primary focus. *What* a student learns and its relationship to material satisfaction becomes more important than *why* the student is learning in the first place. It is this fallacy Newman sought to portray through his use of the fictional senior Mr. Brown.

The first rule of the grammar of Catholic schooling posits the assertion that *why* a student engages in learning is fundamentally more valuable and provides the proper foundation for learning than *what* the student learns. For, without this proper referent, the Catholic community asserts that an educational program voided of its theological dimension is derelict—for it fails to remind students about their ultimate purpose and destiny as God's creatures.

Rule #2: Education is essentially a moral endeavor.

Ante-bellum America certainly was not without its prejudices, not only the blatant racism of the South but also the anti-immigrant and less explicit religious bigotry predominating the North. In crowded urban centers, for example, immigrant Catholic youth attending public schools were compelled to participate in Protestant bible reading and hymn singing. This requirement outraged many Catholics parents, leading them to conclude that public schools were indoctrinating their children in nondenominational Protestantism. In Philadelphia, violent and bloody riots ensued (Lannie & Diethorn, 1968).

Ironically, although the focus of Catholic animus was Protestantism's influence in public schools not religious education *per se*, the social and political consequences engendered by the Philadelphia bible riots forced many public school boards to adopt resolutions expunging religious education from public schools. For the most part, Catholics were steadfast in opposing this compromise, claiming that "education without religion is no education at all." But, as public school boards banned religious education from the nation's public schools, many within the American Catholic community came to the conclusion that they would have to build separate schools if their children were to receive religious education as one element of the standard curriculum.

Evidently, the need to provide Catholic youth a program of religious education had become so serious that, four decades after the deadly riots in Philadelphia and after all avenues to forge a compromise on the issue were exhausted, the bishops at Baltimore III (1884) asserted in their *Pastoral Letter*, "No parish is complete till it has schools adequate to the needs of its children, and the pastor and people of such a parish should feel that they have not accomplished their entire duty until the want is supplied" (Nolan, 1984, p. 225).[1]

Since its issuance, this policy statement has influenced how the American Catholic community views the education of youth. However, of far greater significance than the bishops' mandate that the faithful build Catholic schools is the prophetic vision the bishops included in their policy statement. They wrote to their co-religionists:

> ...education, in order to be sound and to produce beneficial results, must develop what is best in man, and make him not only clever but good. A one-sided education will develop a one-sided life; and such a life will surely topple over, and so will every social system that is built up of such lives. True civilization requires that not only the physical and intellectual, but also the moral and religious, well-being of the people should be promoted, and at least with equal care. Take away religion from a people, and morality would soon follow; morality gone, even their physical condition will ere long degenerate into corruption which breeds decrepitude, while their intellectual attainments would only serve as a light to guide them to deeper depths of vice and ruin....A civilization without religion, would be a civilization of "the struggle for existence, and the survival of the fittest," in which cunning and strength would become the substitutes for principle, virtue, conscience and duty. As a matter of fact, there never has been a civilization worthy of the name without religion.... (Nolan, 1984, p. 223)

This prophecy foretells the deleterious consequences to individuals, communities, and for the nation, too, when religious education is removed from schooling. In light of this prophetic vision, perhaps the true legacy of the Third Baltimore Council is that the nation's bishops formulated for the American Catholic community the second rule of the grammar of Catholic schooling, namely, education is essentially a moral endeavor.

Starratt (1994) uses this grammatical rule as a foundation from which he mounts a stinging criticism of American public schooling. He argues that any reform of 20th-century public schooling must be about remediating the pervasive and debilitating effects of a social ethic that has made it convenient to embrace individualism, stress competition, and inculcate in students those superficial forms of rationality that make students one-dimensional creatures, that is, minds indifferent to the critique of the heart. The outcome of this curriculum, one devoid of a moral foundation, is students who fail to appreciate the value of community and to take seriously their responsibilities to it. Instead, Starratt contends, students learn to conform to external authorities (e.g., peer groups) in the naive belief that this is the proper place to discover their fulfillment. Sadly absent from their decision-making process is a moral base, that is, a substantive framework of norms that will guide and sustain them as adult members having rights and responsibilities in a civic community.

To remedy the disease wrought by a social ethic and educational program devoid of a moral foundation, Starratt challenges public educators to reconceive their craft so as to be about the important business of building ethical schools that offer youth practical experiences of ethical living. In schools which inculcate this moral purpose, Starratt reasons, educators will teach students to think critically, not as an end in itself, but as a means to learn about and to practice puzzling through the moral mazes in which they make decisions about their lives. Students will also practice being just, so that they will not only learn how to engage in self-conscious discourse about the important issues confronting them but will also learn how to make prudential judgments about what they ought to do when confronting moral dilemmas.

Where schooling has this moral foundation, Starratt asserts, care becomes the palpable virtue bonding human beings together as they learn to cooperate with one another in a joint venture called "human life." And, where schooling is this moral endeavor, the entire school community busies itself learning how to care for one another's needs, that virtuous behavior instructing all who practice it to be faithful, to appreciate individual differences, to develop authentic individuality, and to be loyal to one another. Furthermore, where schooling emanates this moral purpose, teachers and students learn to exercise autonomy, connectedness, and transcendence. Ultimately, Starratt maintains, the power exerted by the vices of domination, intimidation, and control will gradually ease as teachers and their students engage in open and trusting communication.

In sum, Starratt challenges public educators to become more attentive to how moral problematics manifest themselves in student behavior. He urges teachers, in particular, to provide healing unctions without reimposing hegemonic control over daily life in schools. Though Starratt did not use the term, he implies that public educators need to

---

Identify how your school emphasizes:
- *individualism;*
- *competition; and,*
- *intellectual prowess.*

Relate these elements of your school's curriculum to its Catholic identity, i.e., how students will learn about and practice Christian personalism.

List three leadership activities you and your faculty can engage in that will transform excessive individualism and competition as well as an exclusive focus on intellectual development into educational experiences inculcating in your school an ethos informed by Christian personalism:

1)_____
2)_____
3)_____

> *Formulate a response to parents who assert that "knowledge is power" and expect your school to stress this objective:*
> _____
> _____
> _____

reinvigorate the "pastoral" dimensions of their craft (i.e., to care for their students' souls as well as their minds and bodies). Otherwise, he asserts, public schools will continue to resemble what they became during the 20th century, that is, organizations uncritically promoting a scientific-rational ideology, wherein schooling focuses exclusively on the transmission of facts and consciously avoids the moral problematics that schools, as communal institutions, are uniquely positioned to remedy.

Standing in contrast to Starratt's critique of 20th century American public schooling and his program for building ethical schools, are those educational reform measures emanating from political discourse that more frequently than not focus upon improving what schools do. The purpose of schooling, from this functionalist perspective, is to convey and assess whether students have acquired the prescribed knowledge and skills that will enable youth to become more useful and productive members of society. "Knowledge is power," is the seductive mantra of those who promote this unmistakably utilitarian ideology. And, power is measured by the scores which students receive on standardized examinations.

With the rise of psychometry in the 20th century, researchers have devised a stunning array of tests to measure the degree to which students have mastered a prescribed curriculum and, by the 1980s, politicians busied themselves in political barnstorming about the need for increased testing at specified periods throughout each student's elementary and secondary school career. These efforts have been successful as "outcomes based education" is now viewed by many citizens as an appropriate tool for the government to use in determining whether and to what degree public school teachers are accomplishing what they have been hired to do, namely, to transmit defined knowledge and skills.[2] Unfortunately, many citizens actually believe SAT scores convey meaningful information about the quality of educational programs when, in fact, the SAT was designed to discriminate a quantity, that is, students who know more from those who know less (D'Souza, 1991).

In contrast to the functionalist, utilitarian ideology that reached its apex with the reform movements of the 1980s and 90s, the grammar of Catholic schooling steadfastly maintains that the substantive mission of educating youth centers around the formation of learning communities which consciously infuse moral norms and experiences into the fabric of education so that these lessons permeate every aspect of student learning. These communities provide students a systematic and lived experience of the values required for responsible adult citizenship in a pluralistic democracy because the development of moral character is the heart of an authentic education and is what makes adults truly useful citizens. As Starratt (1994) points out, schooling involves envisioning a moral framework and inculcating in students the volition necessary to act virtuously.

When education is conceived primarily as a moral endeavor, educators view their work from a normative perspective, in much the same way Plato (1992) described teaching in Book III of the *Republic*. In sum, Plato argued that teachers are "guardians" of civic virtues, that is, Plato viewed teaching as a sacred trust, where women and men embody the community's virtues in their lives, words, and actions. These guardians of the civic virtues challenge youth to actualize these virtues by making them their own. By elevating teaching to a moral sphere, Plato reminds teachers that they devote their lives and talents not only to shaping their students' minds, but more importantly, to shaping the power of their students' will. In this way, one may add, educators participate in an important and necessary pastoral ministry possessing momentous consequences for the civic community.

Pius XII, whose 19-year pontificate spanned three decades (1939-1958), expressed this ideal in a speech he delivered to the executives of the Italian Catholic Union of Secondary Education in 1954:

> ...a Christian instructor cannot be satisfied with teaching techniques. By faith, he knows something which, unfortunately, is confirmed by experience—the importance of sin in the life of the youngster—and he knows the influence of grace as well....He struggles patiently and firmly with the defects of his pupils and trains them in virtue. He lifts them up and improves them. In this way, Christian education participates in the mystery of the Redemption and effectively works with it. From this comes the greatness of your work, which is in a way analogous to that of the priest. (1954a/1979, p. 479)

The grammar of Catholic schooling defines the framework within which education transpires. Because, as the first rule of grammar asserts, God is the beginning and end of human existence, education is essentially a moral endeavor. In particular, this second rule makes morality the fundamental element shaping the education of youth. Without this moral framework, education (that is, "drawing out" the normative framework defining who human beings truly are as God's creatures) is reduced to instruction (that is, "building in" the facts that make one powerful). Schooling youth, then, becomes a functional, utilitarian program rather than substantive sharing of the heritage of civilization.

Ultimately, the grammar of Catholic schooling asks: Of what value is a knowledgeable society that is uninformed about its basic moral obligations? And this grammar resounds: Education is a moral endeavor purposely designed to teach youth about right and wrong, that is, there is a better and a worse way to live one's life and to discover one's fulfillment. Because Catholic education is essentially a moral endeavor, the grammar of Catholic schooling requires educators, in their ministerial role, to be attentive to the formation of the student's soul, even if this must come at the expense of forming the student's intellect. For,

---

- *Reflect on your role and experience as a Catholic school educator.*

- *Identify an experience where you acted as a "guardian of virtue."*

- *List the personal and professional resources this experience required of you.*

- *Design an in-service program for your faculty focusing on these resources and giving clarity to the vocation of the Catholic educator.*

Explore the concepts:

- *teaching as "instruction"*

- *teaching as "education"*

How might you encourage the latter in your teachers?

The Grammar of Catholic Schooling

although the latter is never the ideal, it is far superior to the opposite pedagogical situation, namely, in schools where educators emphasize the formation of their students' intellectual powers at the expense of their souls (Maritain, 1943).

Being an educator in a Catholic school is certainly no easy vocation. Not only does this vocation require magnanimous women and men who allow God's call to transcend their personal and professional decision-making, their vocation also requires these individuals to allow a religious grammar of schooling to inform their deliberations as they consider the substantive issues at the heart of educating youth. Their work involves educating youth, yes. But, as educators in Catholic schools, the Church has charged these magnanimous professionals with a pastoral mission as well: to translate the rules of the grammar of Catholic schooling into a program of moral and intellectual formation for youth.

In sum, the Catholic community entrusts these professionals with the responsibility of immersing youth students in the moral problems manifesting themselves in daily life, both within and outside the school. The educational goal, the outcome of this educational program, is that these young women and men will be able to resolve these problems in a way that is consonant with the accumulated wisdom of the Catholic community. Ultimately, then, this second grammatical rule provides the philosophical rationale by which educators in Catholic schools provide youth an educational program, one that translates human experience into lessons teaching youth how they can and must lead a truly good life, as that good life has been defined by the Catholic community.

Rule #3: Parents are the primary educators of their children.

In 1989, the Carnegie Council on Adolescent Development Task Force released its report detailing the problems associated with educating America's young adolescents. Data revealed that educators, especially teachers of low-income and minority sixth, seventh, and eighth grade students, believe that parents contribute to their student's educational problems. At the same time, these educators also believe that parents are an important resource in ameliorating the problems associated with educating young adolescents. To effect this outcome, the Task Force recommended three avenues for school leaders to encourage greater parental involvement. Namely, principals should: 1) provide parents meaningful roles in school governance; 2) keep parents informed; and, 3) offer families opportunities to encourage and support learning at home and school.

The Carnegie Council's Task Force report provides a focus to consider in greater detail one hotly contested educational issue, namely, parental rights in educating children. It is an issue that has demarcated

---

Vatican II spoke of the Church as the "People of God," emphasizing the individual's relation to and responsibility for the community of God's people.

Identify how the "People of God" metaphor might frame your school's program of moral formation. That is, how does membership in the community of God's people influence and guide your teachers' decision-making process?
1)_____
2)_____
3)_____

Schools are intended to assist parents to fulfill their educational obligations.

Identify how your school might promote this ideal in:
- curriculum development;
- fund-raising and development efforts;
- public relations; and,
- student recruitment.

Catholic from secular educational philosophy for at least 100 years.

In general, Catholic educational philosophy insists that parents are the primary educators of their children. It is a *right* parents possess as a consequence of having participated with God in procreating their children. This right carries with it concomitant responsibilities that parents cannot easily abdicate unless, of course, responsibility for a higher good takes precedence.

In as far as Catholic educational philosophy concerns the state, the Church maintains that the state possesses a legitimate *interest* in educating youth, if for the only reason that an improperly educated citizenry will lead ultimately to the dissolution of the state. The state's interest, however, is of secondary consideration to parental rights, unless of course what parents seek for their children aims toward the destruction of the common good. Thus, in the Catholic schema, parents entrust their children to educators who, as agents of the state, uphold parental rights and responsibilities because these are primary and cannot be abrogated by the state or its agents (except, of course, in extreme circumstances).

In contrast, secular educational philosophy focuses upon the state's role in providing an educational program that will enable its youth to become fully participating and contributing adult members of society. In this schema, parental rights are not *primary*; at best, they are *respected* by the state and its agents. Thus, as this secular philosophy of education relates to public educators, their charge is to implement the educational statutes and policies adopted by the state. At best, educators mediate the state's interests. And, at worst, educators are reduced to functionaries, generic women and men who fill slots in the educational bureaucracy and provide a buffer insulating educators from parents.

During the past century, the fundamental divide in this debate has been the difference between parental rights and state interests. This is no abstract philosophical matter, for it has profound implications governing some very practical matters at the very heart of American public schooling.

For example, eight years after the Carnegie Council on Adolescent Development Task Force issued its report, one of the nation's premiere educational organizations, the Association for Supervision and Curriculum Development (ASCD), proposed a position for its membership focusing on parental rights. The position, debated at the ASCD 1997 Annual Conference, opposed legislation that "would permit legal action against schools officials for 'interfering' with parents' rights to direct the upbringing of their children" (ASCD *Education Update*, 1997, p. 4).

The ASCD proposed position was in response to The Parental Rights and Responsibilities Act (PRRA), an act debated but not enacted by the U.S. Congress in 1996. It would have outlawed any federal, state,

---

Identify five ways that parents are meaningfully involved in your school:
1)_____
2)_____
3)_____
4)_____
5)_____

Cite how parental involvement at your school differs from interference:
_____
_____
_____
_____
_____

How do you handle the inevitable conflict between involvement and interference?

- *At a faculty meeting, lead a discussion among your faculty that examines the Church's stance concerning parental rights.*

- *Have your faculty discuss the challenges the Church's stance on parental rights presents to their professional judgment.*

- *Upholding the primacy of parental rights, develop a process to resolve the conflict that periodically emerges when parental rights conflict with a faculty member's professional judgment.*

- *Reflect upon this process, thinking about it from the perspective that being a Catholic educator is a ministry of service not only to students but also to their parents.*

> **Review your school's mission statement:**
>
> - Does your school's mission statement explicitly state that parents are the primary educators of their children?
>
> - Does your school's mission statement indicate that your school exists to assist parents in fulfilling their educational responsibilities?
>
> - How does your school's mission statement define the proper relationship between home and school?
>
> - Does your school's mission statement suggest a process by which parents and educators might overcome conflict should it arise?
>
> - At a faculty meeting, discuss your findings with your faculty.
>
> - Engage your faculty in rewriting your school's mission statement to make explicit how your school, as a Catholic school, exists to assist those parents who entrust their children to it. Present this written statement to the appropriate governance body for endorsement.

or local government or its agents to interfere with a parent's right to direct the educational program of his or her child. The act, as proposed, would also have granted any parent the right to sue in federal or state court over an alleged violation of the PRRA.

Proponents of the PRRA and other similar statutes and constitutional amendments introduced in more than 24 states argue that governmental bureaucracies, including public schools, interfere with the right of parents to direct the education of their children. Instances that proponents most oftentimes cite include: making condoms readily available to students; exposing students to sexually explicit materials in sex education classes; and, giving counsel and advice to students which violate parental interests.

Taken at face value, most people would accede (along with the National Parent Teachers Association, the National Education Association, and the National School Boards Association) to the principle that school administrators and teachers should not be vulnerable to frivolous objections registered by cranky parents. Likewise, most people would also agree that, for the most part, educators exercise care for students and endeavor to enact the very best possible educational program for them. In this ideal world, only infrequently would educators make erroneous judgments. And, this situation would be rectified quickly as educators and parents consulted and collaborated concerning the particulars of an individual case. Legal protection would be unnecessary.

However, the ASCD's Board of Directors asserts that the reason for raising the issue of parental rights is that today's public educators are torn by multiple loyalties. "We believe that teachers and other *educators should cooperate* with parents and *respect* their wishes as often as feasible. School officials are, however, responsible to the broader community represented by the state the local board of education. Moreover, as professionals, they have a legitimate interest in the welfare of the children they teach" (italics added, p. 4).

From the ASCD's perspective, the focal issue concerns the need for *cooperation* and *respect* between educators and parents. "While we urge respect for parents' rights, we regret the distrust and antagonism that lead to calls for legislation on this matter. Educators and parents both want what they believe is best for children, and neither should act arbitrarily. If differing perspectives cause occasional conflicts, the conflicts should be resolved in a climate of understanding and respect" (p. 4).

Overlooking, for a moment, the fact that the proposed position vitiates the primacy of parental rights and accepts the *de facto* supremacy of the educational bureaucracy, the status parents are accorded by the proposed position fails to accede to parents' equal footing with educators for, were the proposed position to be enacted in states throughout the nation, educators would possess immunity. This raises the question:

How can there be cooperation and respect when one party possesses immunity? For, were physicians to be granted similar immunity, patients across the nation would be barred from suing their doctors for malpractice.

Taken at face value, the proposed position appeals to common sense, especially in a litigious society that revels in frivolous law suits. In reality, however, this position is a less than thinly veiled assault upon parental rights for, by cloaking educators with immunity, the operative premise asserts that educators and state educational bureaucracies know better than parents what is in the best educational interests of children. As one teacher who responded to the ASCD's proposed position opined: "Some parents are afraid their children will be exposed to issues and information that will make them think. When restrictions are placed on a teacher's freedom to teach and all ideas are not free to be understood and learned, we're going back to the Dark Ages" (ASCD *Education Update*, 1997, p. 7).

From a viewpoint informed by the third rule of the grammar of Catholic schooling, the ASCD proposed position is nothing other than a rather disingenuous denigration of parental rights by an educational bureaucracy, whose sole purpose is to increase the state monopoly as this concerns educating youth. In contrast, Catholic educational philosophy steadfastly insists that parents send their daughters and sons to schools because parents seek assistance in educating their children.

However, no matter what type of school parents select for their children, the operative word, from the viewpoint of Catholic educational philosophy, is *assistance*. Because parents, for a variety of reasons, cannot provide their daughters and sons the complete educational program their children require, parents seek the assistance of professional educators who provide for youth what parents cannot. For example, some parents might not be competent to provide their children instruction in physics, trigonometry, or computer programming. Other parents might experience themselves incapable of dealing with the subtleties of grammar and syntax, precision in expository or narrative writing, or interpreting literature. And, some parents also seek the assistance of educators who provide their daughters and sons an environment that supports and encourages parental moral values as well as instructs youth in parental religious beliefs and attitudes.

Given the self-protective organizational structure that the grammar of public schooling erects, it becomes rather difficult for people to conceive of a system of public schooling that would be responsive to parental rights. Imagine, for a moment, a public school whose mission it is to be responsive to parents by providing the assistance they seek in educating their daughters and sons. Why is this difficult to imagine? And, why is it difficult to translate into actual practice? Perhaps this is because, in the United States at least, educating youth is a very big

---

Catholic educational philosophy specifies the proper relationship between home, Church, and state:

HOME: *parental rights are primary (a divine right that cannot be abrogated)*

CHURCH: *the Church possesses an interest in the moral formation of youth (as citizens of God's kingdom)*

STATE: *the state possesses an interest in the intellectual formation of youth (as citizens of a secular nation)*

The interests of the Church and State take precedence to parental rights only in those cases where parents are derelict in their moral or civic obligations.

Further, because education concerns the student's soul (and this involves eternal life), the Church's interest takes precedence to the State's interest (which involves mortal life).

business that stands independent of the communities that schools serve. While standardization may have had the positive impact of making schooling more efficient, standardization may also have had the negative impact of insulating schools and those who labor in them from the parents and communities that schools are designed to assist.

Sarason (1995) comes at the question of parental rights from a perspective differing from both the grammar of Catholic schooling and that articulated by the ASCD in its proposed position. Sarason maintains that the "political principle" inherent in the governance structure of American public schools makes it impossible for educators to express their heartfelt care for students, particularly in those instances where educators may make judgments conflicting with parental interests. To ameliorate situations where parental involvement and the political principle make it impossible for parents and educators to collaborate toward the goal of educating youth, Sarason asserts that the existing governance structure of public schools (one dimension of what Tyack and Tobin have called "the grammar of public schooling") be abolished.

Standing in stark contrast to recommendations like those issued by the Carnegie Council on Adolescent Development Task Force, policy proposals like those debated by the ASCD, or the more radical suggestions of critics like Sarason, the third rule of the grammar of Catholic schooling makes explicit who bears primary responsibility for educating youth: *Parents are the primary educators of their children.* It is not for educators to determine when, where, and how parents will be meaningfully involved in school governance. Nor is it for school leaders to define those avenues through which parents might involve themselves in the education of their children. Nor should principals and teachers possess immunity for the erroneous educational decisions they make. Instead, the third rule of the grammar of Catholic schooling serves to remind parents that it is *they* who bear the moral obligation to determine just when, where, and how *educators* will become involved in the education of their children. When parental rights are interfered with, parents possess the moral obligation to act even if that were to mean initiating legal action against educators. Finally, politics is not the bane of public schooling, as critics like Sarason assert. Rather, a defective philosophy of parental rights and educator responsibilities is.

Though the third rule of this grammar has roots winding their way deep into Catholic theology and philosophy, this rule was clarified in Church documents at least as early as 1887, when Leo XIII (1887/1971) wrote the encyclical, *Officio sanctissimo*. In that letter, Leo XIII set forth the rights and duties of parents, the Church, and the State as each concerns the education of youth. In retrospect, *Officio* provided the normative framework in the late-19th and early 20th-centuries from which U.S. Catholic educational policy took its shape.

Officio sanctissimo asserts that the duties and rights of parents

---

Make plans for next year's Catholic Schools Week to include educational activities for parents to learn about their rights in educating their children. Some activities and topics could include:

The homily at Sunday Mass: "The primacy of parental rights and their moral obligation in educating their children."

A one-hour, evening seminar for parents hosted by your faculty: "Our efforts to assist you to provide your children a moral and intellectual formation."

A brochure mailed to parents: "Meaningful parental involvement in the education of your children."

in the education of youth are primarily moral—an obligation binding parents to educate their children in the knowledge of religion and good habits, as well as piety toward God. While parents bear a natural obligation to support their children's general growth and development, they also bear a more important moral obligation, namely, to bring their children up in the life of the soul, i.e., their spiritual life. Parents, Leo XIII argues, assume these grave responsibilities as a direct consequence of freely participating in the procreation of their children. Because the duties resulting from having children are of a divine origin, emerging from the bond uniting the child's parents and God,

> [parents] cannot easily surrender them to any human authority nor can any human power usurp them. If parents do delegate others to provide for the education of their children, they arc courting disaster, when, with great peril, they entrust their children, easily deceived and defenseless as these are, to teachers who are suspect...If [parents] themselves cannot ensure [that their children receive a proper religious education], they must allow themselves to be substituted, but in such a manner that the children receive and learn the necessary religious doctrine from approved teachers. (p. 106)

The Church also bears an interest in educating youth, namely, that they receive spiritual (i.e., moral) training. In those regions of the world where moral training cannot be a part of the regular educational program, for example, in those nations where children are required to attend religiously neutral state schools, Leo XIII maintained, Catholic parents might have to open "their own schools at the cost of great self-sacrifice and expense..." (p. 107).

Leo XIII's wording here is significant, particularly for the U.S. Catholic Church whose history is one where the institutional Church has aggressively established separate schools. Leo XIII suggests, however, not that the Church establishes these schools (a familiar theme for U.S. Catholics), but that the Catholic faithful establish these schools. His assertion raises an important question: Just who really sponsors Catholic schools? Is it the institutional Church, sensing a threat to its authority in the moral life of the faithful, which first establishes schools and then requires parents to send their children to them? Or, is it because of the fact that state-supported schools do not provide for the students' spiritual perfection and parents must see to it that "youth do not run any risk or suffer any harm to the Catholic faith or to the integrity of their morals" (Leo XIII, 1887/1971, p. 106)? If the latter is the case, it is Catholic parents, functioning as the primary educators of their children, who charter these schools and enlist educators to aid them in providing the proper education for their children.

In *Officio sanctissimo*, Leo XIII also asserted that the State possesses an interest in the education of youth. This interest arises from

---

Identify the five "risks" you see threatening your students:
1)_____
2)_____
3)_____
4)_____
5)_____

List how your school explicitly deals with each risk identified above:
1)_____
2)_____
3)_____
4)_____
5)_____

In light of the risks and your school's response, define what you mean by the term "educational reform."

If you were to reform your school's educational program, what would you do to see to it that your school's educational program ameliorates the risks posed to your students?

the fact that the State, in order to assure its survival and perfection, needs an educated adult citizenry that is capable of upholding and promoting the common good. But, Leo XIII argues, it is the Christian religious education of youth not a purely secular educational program that will effect the State's perfection:

> It is clear that many serious evils are to be feared for a society in which the program and method of instruction do not include religion, or, what is worse, oppose it. Once we neglect and despise that supreme and divine authority, which teaches respect for the authority of God and confirms the certainty of our faith in divine revelation human science moves to swift destruction, deteriorating into pernicious errors, beginning with naturalism and rationalism. (p. 107)

When an educational program does not inculcate the respect for God's authority as well as that of the State, "the social bond that binds men is broken and destroyed; there will be no longer any public well-being and all will be subject to the tyranny of force and crime" (p. 107).

According to *Officio sanctissimo*, the proper ordering of educational rights and responsibilities exhibits an harmonious relationship uniting parents, the Church, and the state in a cooperative venture which aims at cultivating each child's moral and intellectual capacities. In this schema, parental rights and responsibilities to provide for the moral and intellectual development of their children are supported by the Church and the civil state. In short, there is and should be no conflict. And, as a consequence, where parents, in good conscience, provide a religious education for their children at home or in a public school, there exists no need to provide a nonpublic school.

It was this view of parental rights that the Church codified in the 1919 Code of Canon Law: "Parents are under a grave obligation to see to the religious and moral education of their children, as well as to their physical and civic training, as far as they can, and moreover to provide for their temporal well-being" (CIC I.100.113). This law was to have far-reaching impact, particularly in the United States, where it was used by pastors not only to remind parents of their obligations but also in some instances to coerce parents to send their children to parochial schools.

Forty-two years after the issuance of *Officio sanctissimo*, Pius XI (1929/1979) delineated the third rule of the grammar of Catholic schooling in his encyclical, *On The Christian Education of Youth*. Using scholastic philosophy to support his thesis, Pius XI reiterated and expanded upon Leo XIII's assertion about the three societies interested in the education of youth as well as the rights and responsibilities assigned to each. Assigning primary responsibility for the education of youth to the sociological unit of the family "...instituted directly by God for its peculiar purpose, the procreation and formation of offspring; for this reason it has priority of nature and therefore of rights over civil society" (p. 204), the pontiff argued that parental rights are also anterior to those of the Church: "God directly communicates to the family, in the natural order" (p. 212).

It was this particular view that the U.S. Supreme Court sustained in *Pierce v. Society of Sisters* (268 U.S. 510, 1925). Responding to a challenge to a 1922 Oregon initiative requiring all children between the ages of eight and sixteen to attend public school by 1926 (the only exceptions being children who were mentally or physically unfit, or who had completed the eighth grade, or who had received private instruction from a parent or private teacher with the written permission of the county superintendent of schools), the Court noted that the question raised by *Pierce* had nothing to do with Oregon's power to reasonably regulate schools within its jurisdiction. Instead, the Court focused upon the imbalance in interests introduced by *Pierce*.[3] The Court upheld the notion that the fundamental theory of liberty upon which all governments in this Union repose excludes any general power of the state to standardize its children by forcing them to accept instruction from public teachers only:

> *The child is not the mere creature of the state*; those who nurture him and direct his destiny have the right couple with the high duty to recognize and prepare him for additional obligations. (italics added)

Noting that the child is not the mere creature of the state and subject solely to its legislative fiats, the Court recognized and affirmed the existence of parental rights in educational matters. Far from conferring a right on parents, the Court recognized it as an *a priori* and curbed the power of states like Oregon to encroach upon and to defy parental rights concerning the type of school parents want their children to attend. However, while *Pierce* curbed the states' power states to monopolize educational opportunity, the decision failed to tip the balance in favor of parental rights by requiring states to provide the particular type of educational program that parents might desire for their children. Instead, parental rights and state interests were to remain in a delicate balance with neither gaining ascendancy over the other.

Nearly five decades later, Arons (1976) reassessed *Pierce*, examining its implications for schooling in the United States. Arons developed his argument from the notion that all education, whether secular or religious, involves inculcating certain values in students. Thus, because there exists no such thing as value-neutral education, either in religious or secular schools, Arons reasons, "the form of compulsory schooling chosen by the state has profound and, in some cases, unconstitutional implications for the preservation of freedom of expression, as well as for the freedom of value formation which underlie the First Amendment" (p. 79).

Catholic schools provide students an "integral education," one joining academic achievement and virtuous citizenship.

List three ways your school honors your students' academic achievements (the matters of the mind):
1)_____
2)_____
3)_____

List three ways your school honors virtuous citizenship on the part of your students (the matters of the heart):
1)_____
2)_____
3)_____

Do you find an imbalance present? If so, what steps must you take to insure that your school provides students an integral formation?

Arons uses this premise to launch into a detailed argument against a narrow interpretation of *Pierce* asserting that the neutrality mandated by the First Amendment is safeguarded solely in the situation where parents are given a "maximum practicable choice of schooling for their children" (1976, p. 78). Contrasting this standard against a broader interpretative standard, Arons argues that it is unconstitutional for the government to demand that parents sacrifice their rights (as guaranteed by *Pierce*) as the price they must pay for free public schooling. Furthermore, Arons argues that it is also unconstitutional for the state to demand that parents sacrifice their earnings (in the form of tuition payments) to send their children to a religious school that is not value-neutral as the price they must pay to exercise their rights. Simply put: the alleged choice guaranteed by a narrow interpretation of *Pierce* does not satisfy the principle of government neutrality toward parental choice in education.

Conflict results when, for example, a strict wall of separation is erected by a government, whether federal or state, which defines education from a value-laden secularist ethic and thereby arbitrarily denies parents their divine right to educate their children as they see fit, as if parents possess only those educational rights and responsibilities accorded them by the state. For parents who have the economic means, they can opt out of a totalitarian educational system that strips them of their fundamental rights.

But, many rightfully wonder, "What about the poor who do not have liberty to educate their children in any school of their choice, or in any way they wish?" Ravitch (1994) responds:

> *somebody's children* are compelled—one might say condemned—to attend schools that 'should never be called schools at all.' *Somebody's children* go to those schools. Not mine. Not yours. Not the Secretary's. Not the President's nor the Vice President's. Surely not the Mayor's nor the Superintendent's nor even the teachers'. What would the best and wisest parents do if their children were zoned into schools that are physically unsafe and educationally bankrupt? They would move to a different neighborhood or put their children into private schools. That's what the President and the Vice-President did. That is what well-to-do and middle-class parents do.
>
> But *somebody's children* are required to go to those schools. Somebody who doesn't have the money to move to a better neighborhood or to put their child into a private school has been told that their child must stay there no matter how bad the school is. If they are parents with motivation and energy, they are told by school officials and policymakers that they must stay right where they are, because they are the kind of parents who might someday help to improve that dreadful school. The people who tell them this would not keep their own child in that school for even a day. (pp. 3-4)

In response to these and other similar situations, concerned Catholic citizens like Quade (1996) have become more politically active. And, to their credit, these efforts have borne fruit, for example, by convincing legislators in Wisconsin and the mayor of Milwaukee that educating youth should be a parental *choice*. In some locales, children are no longer compelled to attend the public school or to undertake a state-mandated curriculum that does not reflect parental wishes.

Many well-intentioned citizens who support Quade's political approach to redress the balance have become active in seeking legislative relief in the form of tuition tax-credits and educational vouchers. However, when viewed through the prism provided by the grammar of Catholic schooling, Quade's assertion that parental choice should be legalized presumes that the state already possesses the authority to give parents a choice about something they already possess as an inalienable right. Unfortunately, line-of-reasoning reflects a lack of familiarity with the fundamental rules of the grammar of Catholic schooling, a "haziness of intellectual vision" (Newman, 1927, p. 346) that further legitimates the state's gradual but sure usurpation of parental and responsibilities by selectively ignoring the standard articulated by the U.S. Supreme Court in *Pierce*.

According to the grammar of Catholic schooling, parental rights and obligations, as these concern educating their children, are God-given. Parental rights must be upheld and supported by the Church and the State, for the healthy moral and intellectual development of the most important national treasure, God's children.

Rule #4: The subject is the student.

Debate concerning the allegedly precarious condition of the nation's schools, particularly as that debate became focused in the years following the issuance of *A Nation at Risk* (National Commission on Educational Excellence, 1983), provides a framework to clarify another essential difference demarcating the grammar of public schooling from the grammar of Catholic schooling.

In *A Nation at Risk*, as well as in the ensuing tidal wave of rhetoric about the reform of American public education stirred up by the report, the educational "risk" confronting the nation was a concept abstracted from the scores students achieved on quantitative testing instruments designed to identify what students actually did and did not know. While the scores that students achieved did allow for meaningful comparisons to be made and tentative conclusions to be drawn, at least one assumption implicitly guided how the reformers interpreted the data, namely, that the technology driving the multi-billion dollar American educational industry is curriculum and instruction.

Though the lapse in student achievement promulgated by the educational reformers could have been a consequence of a multitude of

The Grammar of Catholic Schooling

> **Several times each week, walk through your school being careful to observe each of the classrooms:**
>
> - Identify those instances where teachers are encouraging in their students a delight of learning.
>
> - When you return to your office, write down your observations, citing: the teacher, pedagogical method, names of students, etc.
>
> - Place these observations in the teacher's file.
>
> - At evaluation time, share each of these observation with the faculty member.
>
> - At an academic honors ceremony, relate these stories to the audience.
>
> - At graduation, tell the assembly about the "virtuous women and men" who form your school's faculty.

confounding factors, many reformers forged ahead to remedy the ailing public educational system. Possessing an unbridled belief in the infinite perfectibility of educational technology, these reformers reasoned that better curriculum and improved instructional methods would inevitably lead to improved student outcomes on standardized tests and, as a result, demonstrate increased school effectiveness. To fix the problem evidencing itself in the scores students received on standardized measures as well as to remediate the risk that educational failure posed to the nation, various reform schemes were hatched to improve educational technology. Some of these schemes were eventually legislated.

One predominant strand of reform schemes took dead aim at teachers. Some legislatures designed plans to identify excellent teachers. These exemplars would then work with their less capable peers so that the latter could learn from and imitate the expertise of the former. For example, some states adopted mentorship and peer coaching programs that gave effective teachers reduced instructional loads or release time to share their expertise with novice teachers, to work with individual teachers experiencing difficulties teaching students, or to challenge burned-out veteran teachers who desperately needed to recharge their pedagogical repertoire. Several states legislated career ladders to reward effective teachers for their efforts and to penalize those failing to develop professionally. Most states mandated some form of continuing education for teachers to renew their instructional certificates.

This strand of reform measures were, for the most part, stop-gap measures designed to improve the technical skills of the current pool of teachers. In the meantime, universities, colleges and departments of education would prepare the next generation of teachers. These women and men, then, would possess the most technologically advanced pedagogical training and, once certified, would replace ineffective teachers currently populating classrooms throughout the nation. A few states, Pennsylvania among them, offered one-time "golden parachutes" to lure ineffective teachers out of their classrooms and into the pastures of a leisurely retirement. Thus, to facilitate reform, most states revised the certification process and incorporated additional requirements for aspiring teachers (and administrators as well) before they would enter schools to begin practicing their craft.

A second prominent strand of reform schemes took aim at students. The reasoning behind many of the plans hatched in state legislatures appealed to what was, for many, obvious. The legislators asked: Aren't students supposed to master the basic rudiments of an academic curriculum? And: Why should students participate in the school's extra-curriculum if they fail the academic curriculum?

In response to these rather common sense questions, many state legislatures began to mandate that all students demonstrate proficiency on criteria-referenced tests administered at various grade levels throughout the elementary and secondary years, particularly in math and science. Other states swiftly enacted laws to increase their promotion and graduation requirements. The era of the "shopping mall" high school (Powell, Farrar, & Cohen, 1985) came to a screeching halt. The Texas state legislature became somewhat of a *cause celèbre* when it legislated a "No Pass, No Play" law. It was a simple reform, appealing to common sense. In brief, the law mandates that students who do not pass their courses will not be allowed to participate in extra-curricular activities.[4] All the while, curricular reform (which, for the public at large and for many politicians as well, denoted a "return to the basics") remained the purview of those who controlled state legislatures.

At its zenith, the reform movement spawned by *A Nation at Risk* found the President of the United States gathering the nation's 50 governors at historic Williamsburg, Virginia, to develop a national reform strategy. That the chief executive officer of the federal government, George Bush, had convened a meeting of the nation's governors about a matter constitutionally reserved to the states was unprecedented. But, with the nation "committing an act of unthinking, unilateral educational disarmament" (National Commission on Educational Excellence, 1983, p. 5), many concerned citizens entertained the vague hope that the bully-pulpit of the Presidency would motivate the nation's governors to fashion a consensus concerning how to best educate American youth for the 21st century.

As the reform movement clarified the term "reform" in the wake of *A Nation at Risk*, the subject of public schooling was increasingly equated with the curriculum and instructional methods teachers used to convey what students should know in order to function effectively as literate and contributing adult citizens in the 21st century. Throughout the debate, effective teaching was made synonymous with instructional methods while learning was defined as mastering the bits and scraps of information that would be assessed intermittently on state-mandated tests.[5]

When the subject of schooling is reduced to matters of curriculum and instruction, pedagogical expertise becomes focal. Identifying expert teachers is simplified: they are those instructors who possess an intangible love for the subject matter they teach as well as the ability to communicate this enthusiasm to their students. The highest compliment that can be paid to this dedicated public servant comes forth from the mouths of parents whose student demonstrates interest in the subject taught by that instructor, especially as that effect is measured on standardized instruments. How many parents, for example, have boasted to their relatives, neighbors, co-workers, and even the school's principal about a particular teacher who helped their child to master vocabulary or concepts of science, history, and language so that she scored exceptionally well on the SAT examination and was accepted into her first

---

During the first semester, walk through your school periodically each week, keenly observing the predominant teaching model present in each classroom.

Note your observations on a chart:
Date: _____
Time of Day : _____
Classroom: _____
Teacher: _____

Predominant Teaching Model:
_____ teacher-centered
_____ student-centered
_____ active learning
_____ passive learning

At the end of the first semester, summarize your findings and report them to your faculty. Engage your faculty in a discussion about pedagogical methods and their function as a tool (the educational means) to form youth (the educational end).

Repeat the process during the second semester. Report changes to your faculty. Engage your faculty in thinking about expanding their pedagogical repertoire. At evaluation time, challenge your faculty to experiment with new methods, perhaps identifying another teacher who could serve as a coach/mentor.

college-of-choice? Likewise, how many parents (like Newman's senior Mr. Brown) bemoan their son's or daughter's rejection at a college of first choice by condemning teachers and administrators or the college's acceptance standards and admissions procedures?

For those educated according to the grammar of Catholic schooling, these self-aggrandizing and prideful compliments ring hollow, for they reduce the teacher to the status of a "word vendor," an appellation decried early in the fifth century by Augustine of Hippo (*Confessions* IV.2). Having himself enjoyed wide repute as a masterful teacher of rhetoric, Augustine sarcastically inquired in his work *On the Teacher* (*de Magistro*), "For who would be so absurdly curious as to send his child to school to learn what the teacher thinks?" (1949, p. 185). When reformers and educators focus solely upon the educational means, curriculum and instruction, those who should know better lose sight of the *a priori* educational end, that is, the formation of an authentic and genuine human being, the educational "product" as it were.

In fact, *A Nation at Risk* (1983) expressed a profound concern about the *a priori* end of education, particularly in the much overlooked paragraph where the Commission stated:

> Our concern, however, goes well beyond matters such as industry and commerce. It also includes the *intellectual, moral, and spiritual* strengths of our people which knit together the very fabric of our society....A high level of shared education is essential to a free, democratic society and to the fostering of a common culture, especially in a country that prides itself on pluralism and individual freedom. (p. 7, italics added)

Although most of the previous decade's educational reform efforts made common sense, these efforts have not dealt as effectively with the root causes of the nation's educational risk as they have taken aim at its symptoms, that is, teachers, students, and curricula.

Small pockets of interest in having educators and the school's curriculum address the moral dimension of human experience and its importance for youth have slowly emerged. In 1993, the American Educational Research Association (AERA) constituted a special interest group (SIG), Moral Development in Education, which expands research beyond that being done by an existing AERA-SIG, Religion and Education. Also, the prominent periodical for school administrators, *Educational Leadership*, devoted two issues to related topics, character education (November 1993) and Christian fundamentalism (December 1993/January 1994). In addition, the School of Education at the State University of New York at Geneseo has offered an elective course for graduate education majors, "Religion and the Public Schools" (Yob, 1994). An American Academy of Religion SIG is devoted to introducing religious studies courses into public school curricula. Unfortunately, each of these efforts has equated the means (educational technology) with the ends (functioning as a moral human being), seeking to introduce the study of these themes into public school curriculum and instruction. As Carr (1991) astutely notes in his book concerning the philosophical psychology of moral development and education, "educating the virtues" differs radically from "educating about the virtues."

One of the more provocative efforts to make the student the subject of schooling stems from the work not of an educator, a theologian, or a politician, but that of a sociologist, Amitai Etzioni. In *The Spirit of Community*, Etzioni (1993) advocates the rights, responsibilities, and agenda shared by the Communitarian movement. In his book, Etzioni argues that the American nation must be reawakened to the notion of community and an allegiance to the shared values and institutions that sustain a commonweal. Extending the implications of his argument to marriages, families, neighborhoods, and schools, Etzioni emphasizes the basic principles of the democratic social contract and the moral responsibilities incumbent upon all individuals who wish to be part of that community.

In particular, Etzioni argues, the "Communitarian school" is charged with dealing "extensively with personality development and the introduction of values" (p. 89). By personality development, Etzioni means shaping the student's character by helping him to learn "the capacity to control one's impulses and to mobilize oneself for acts other than the satisfaction of biological needs and immediate desires" (p. 91). The intention of this training is to enable students to control their impulses, defer gratification, and experience the self-rewarded feeling for having done what is right and having avoided what is wrong.

"What is important?", Etzioni asks. Unflinchingly, he responds:

> ...[T]he single most important factor that affects education from within the schools is neither the curriculum nor the teaching style, at least not as these terms are normally used, but the experiences the school generates....It is almost certainly a good place to start the reconstruction of the schools as *educational* institutions if they are to become places where *self*-discipline is evolved. Otherwise schools will not only fail their graduates, they will also be unable to serve as a major foundation of the moral infrastructure of our communities. (italics in text, p. 115)

Though Etzioni's argument rings true, it is not at all new. In fact, it was nearly 65 years ago that Pius XI (1929/1979) surveyed the state of education throughout the world and issued what came to be known as the "Magna Carta of Catholic Education," *Divini illius Magistri*, that is, "The Education of the Redeemed." "Indeed never has there been so much discussion about education as nowadays," Pius XI wrote the faithful, "...never have exponents of new pedagogical theories been so

---

Catholic schools are community schools, where students learn to exercise their rights and responsibilities.

Cite instances where you see your students learning to:

• *control their impulses*

_____
_____
_____
_____

• *experience self-reward for doing what is right and avoiding what is wrong*

_____
_____
_____

Use these instances to tell a story about learning in your school (e.g., at an open house for new parents, at an assembly or pep rally, at graduation).

numerous, or so many methods and means devised, proposed and debated, not merely to facilitate education, but to create a new system infallibly efficacious, and capable of preparing the present generations for that earthly happiness which they so ardently desire" (pp. 201-202). But, the Pope insisted, "instead of fixing their attention on God, the first principle and last end of the entire universe, they fall back upon themselves, become attached exclusively to the passing things of this earth..." (p. 202).

Standing in stark opposition to the notion that the subject of education is the curriculum and the instructional methods utilized to convey it, the fourth rule of the grammar of Catholic schooling maintains that the student is the subject of schooling. Pius XI codified the rule in this way:

> It should never be forgotten that the subject of Christian education is man as a whole, soul united by body by nature, together with all his faculties, natural and supernatural, such as right reason and revelation show him to be; man, fallen from his original estate, but redeemed by Christ and restored to the supernatural condition of adopted [child] of God.... (1929/1979, p. 227)

Catholic educational philosophy insists that the proper focus of all curriculum and instruction is the unique, individual human being. The subject of education is the child sent each day by her parents to a school where she undertakes the moral and intellectual program that her parents trust will effect desired outcomes concerning not only what their child will know, understand, and value but also how their child as an adult member of society will use what she has come to know, understand, and value as a consequence of the educational program she received.

In short, the teleological end of Catholic schooling is the formation of an authentic human being. Primary pedagogical emphasis is placed upon using every available curricular and instructional resource to assist students to overcome those personal defects which keep each of them from becoming fully functioning moral and intellectual beings. "It is therefore as important to make no mistake in education, as it is to make no mistake in the pursuit of the last goal, with which the whole work of education is intimately and necessarily connected," Pius XI (1929/1979) wrote. "In fact, since education consists essentially in preparing man for what he must be and for what he must do here below, in order to attain the sublime goal for which he was created, it is clear that there can be no true education which is not wholly directed to man's last end...." (pp. 202-203).

Developing the pedagogical implications of this rule of grammar perhaps better than any educational philosopher of the 20th century, Maritain dissented from the pervasive 20th century functional paradigm, asserting that education must be concerned more with substantive goals than techniques and more with developing a whole human being than focusing exclusively on aptitudes. In *Education at the Crossroads*, Maritain (1943) explicated four fundamental norms to guide teachers whose subject is the student.

Maritain's first norm specifies that teachers "foster those fundamental dispositions which enable the [student] to grow in the life of the mind" (p. 39). Contrasting this activity to animal training, Maritain argues that, while liberating the student's intellectual powers does sometimes necessitate teachers to suppress their students' bad tendencies, the art of pedagogy requires more, namely, bringing to the students' conscious awareness their individual resources and potential for experiencing the delight of learning. In Maritain's view, it is this desire that motivates the power of the will to overcome bad tendencies and, as the power of the intellect is empowered, students develop the strength to pursue the questions challenging them in their deepest spirit. In short, Maritain advocates that teachers inculcate self-discipline in their students. By this he does not mean using excessive punitive disciplinary measures (especially as caricatures of Catholic schooling have distorted the reality), for Maritain reminds teachers that encouragement facilitates intellectual growth while humiliation can be debilitating.

Maritain's second norm requires teachers to center their students' attention upon how their educational experiences are being internalized. That is, "[b]efore being formed and expressed in concepts and judgments, intellectual knowledge is at first a beginning of insight, still unformulated which proceeds from the impact of the illuminating activity of the intellect on the world of images and emotions and which is but a humble and trembling movement yet invaluable, toward an intelligible content to be grasped" (p. 41). As students become aware of the internal dynamism that is present within them, teachers can gradually awaken and liberate their students' intuitive powers and creativity. Maritain argues:

> If a teacher himself is concerned with discerning and seeing, with getting vision, rather than with collecting facts and opinions, and if he handles his burden of knowledge so as to see through it into the reality of things, then in the mind of the student the power of intuition will be awakened and strengthened unawares, by the very intuitivity traversing such teaching. (p. 45)

Maritain's third norm suggests that "the whole work of education and teaching must tend to unify, not to spread out; it must strive to foster internal unity in man" (p. 45). Maritain presumed that youth are besieged by many diverse interests and drives, all of which constantly vie for attention. In this sense, youth are enslaved by their interests and drives to the degree they do not experience an internal unity in all that they are learning. Teachers, whose proper subject is their students, help

Identify the core values predominating your school's formal and informal curriculum:

_____
_____
_____
_____
_____

Are these values any different than the values taught in Catholic schools of previous generations? If so, why?

The Grammar of Catholic Schooling

them to foster internal unity, what Newman (1927) called "comprehensive understanding," by equipping their students' minds with an ordered knowledge that will enable them to advance toward wisdom in adulthood. For Maritain, it is not only necessary for students to learn facts; they must also be able to conceive how the facts coalesce. Then student will be able to form accurate generalizations about the true nature of things and to act rightly upon them.

Finally, Maritain's fourth norm requires teachers to liberate their students' minds by emphasizing the power of reason over the power of factual recall. Sounding like John Dewey (1916/1944), an early advocate of active learning, Maritain emphasizes that curricula "should never be passively or mechanically received, as dead information which weighs down and dulls the mind. Instead, the mind must rather be actively transformed by understanding into the very life of them, and thus strengthen the latter...." (p. 50). Teachers utilize the facts associated with their disciplines as the foundation from which to help students learn to reason about those facts.

As Maritain's educational philosophy illustrates, when the subject of schooling is the student, conceptions about teachers and teaching are transformed. No longer are teachers functionaries contracted by school districts. Nor are teachers objective and dispassionate professionals trained to implement prescribed curriculum and instructional methods. Instead, teachers engage in their profession in the first place because they possess a profound respect for and love of youth. And, these teachers experience their deepest satisfaction as they devote their life's energies to help youth confront their God-given purpose in life. Furthermore, where the subject of education is the student, curriculum and instruction become the pedagogical tools through which teachers make incarnate the love of God for His children, a love that dwells abundantly in the hearts of those educators who have dedicated their lives to the formidable and arduous ministry of educating youth.

Because the proper subject of Catholic education is the student, a teacher's genius is evident not so much in the way she functions in her classroom as a technical expert in pedagogical matters. Neither is her genius evident in the scores her students receive on standardized achievement tests. Instead, as this teacher concerns herself with fashioning wise human beings who will become the next generation's adults citizens, her genius becomes evident as she makes creative use of the tools of her profession to craft environments and experiences that mediate a particular viewpoint concerning the purpose for and proper end of human existence. This teacher is an "educational connoisseur" (Eisner, 1985) who utilizes the resources she has at hand, limited as these may be, to craft a classroom that embodies the school's culture and forms the next generation's moral and intellectual leaders.

It is this ideal which defines the true subject of Catholic educa-

---

Sergiovanni (1995) argues that teacher excellence is predicated by teacher competence.

Teacher competencies include:
- *basic classroom management skills;*
- *good human relations skills; and,*
- *pedagogical and curriculum skills.*

As teachers build upon these competencies, excellence becomes evident in:
- *the skilled and creative use of the symbolic to communicate the school's purpose; and,*
- *the effective communication of the school's culture.*

As you reflect about your faculty, do you spend the majority of your supervisory practice directed at promoting teacher competence or excellence?

tion: the student. What else could possibly motivate women and men to devote themselves to the largely thankless, in all too many places underpaid, and oftentimes forgotten pastoral ministry of inculcating in youth the important knowledge, skills, and values that will enable them to become, as adults, fully functioning creatures of God who will act as His disciples through His power and in His name?

Thus, in as far as the technology of Catholic schooling is concerned, curriculum and instruction are the primary means for educating students in their rights and responsibilities as God's creatures. The curriculum includes everything that pertains to the student's well-being, including their physical, intellectual, social, psychological, and moral growth, so that they will be well-prepared through the process of schooling to lead their lives based upon the clear, sure, and profound "conviction, firm as a rock, of absolute truth, of the divine force of that faith from which all the rest receives life and value" (Pius XII, 1949/1979, p. 371). The functional aspects of instructing students are primarily a matter of crafting the curriculum to relate what a student learns to what the student is called to become as a creature of God. In this schema, the *a priori* substantive educational ends inform the functional means to those ends.

Since the early 1990s, Thomas Lickona, a Catholic who is a developmental psychologist and professor of education at State University of New York at Cortland, has been heralding the importance of character education and its centrality in the public school curriculum. Arguing that public schools oftentimes are more reactive when addressing the problems of youth than being proactive in combating their underlying causes, Lickona urges that public educators must teach youth right from wrong as well as civic virtues like Lickona's 4th and 5th R's, respect and responsibility.

Lickona's (1991) 12-point comprehensive approach to character education is really about changing public school culture as well as what schools teach. For example, Lickona would have schools devote a segment of each school day to discuss the "virtue of the week" and teachers would make this virtue explicit by integrating examples of it into their courses. Lickona would also have teachers and students address complex and controversial moral issues in a sustained and serious way so that students will develop their capacity to make responsible and moral decisions.

Although Lickona's ideas regarding character education are steeped in Catholic educational philosophy, they are not sectarian. Perhaps his most controversial assertion, namely, that there exist "right" decisions steeped in virtue (versus "wrong" decisions steeped in vice), has made Lickona a favorite target of those whose approach to character education would heartily encourage students to debate the worth of values themselves. For Lickona, however, the virtues he advocates be

---

Cite how your school, as a Catholic educational community, focuses on the following virtues Lickona associates with good citizenship:

respect:
a) _____
b) _____
c) _____

responsibility:
a) _____
b) _____
c) _____

Use your end-of-year faculty meeting to identify the values your school will focus on in the coming academic year. Encourage your teachers to include these virtues in their instructional plans.

inculcated in students, the qualities of character he believes need to be infused throughout the curriculum (e.g., respect, responsibility), are not debatable. Why? Because these virtues are universally accepted.

It is Lickona's stance on the universal validity of certain values that troubles some secular theorists. For example, in a sharply critical rejoinder, Alfie Kohn (1997) argues that what is wrong with most character education programs, especially narrow programs that focus on sex education, is that these programs are "designed to make children work harder and do what they're told" (p. 429). "Character education rests on three ideological legs: behaviorism, conservatism, and religion. Of these, the third raises the most delicate issues for a critic, it is here that the charge of *ad hominem* argument is most likely to be raised," Kohn argues, adding,

> so let us be clear: it is of no relevance that almost all of the leading proponents of character education are devout Catholics. But it is entirely relevant that, in the shadows of their writings, there lurks the assumption that only religion can serve as the foundation for good character....It is appropriate to consider the personal beliefs of these individuals are ensconced in the movement they have defined and directed. What they do on Sundays is their own business, but if they are turning our public schools into Sunday schools, that's everyone's business. (p. 436)

But, that is the precise issue: educating the character of the nation's youth is everyone's business, especially in a nation evidencing the effects of virtueless behavior—teenage sexual irresponsibility, the rising tide of youth violence, increasing dishonesty, and declining civic responsibility. Character education is not a matter driven by "a stunningly dark view of children—and people in general" (Kohn, 1997, p. 431) where "teaching is a matter of telling and compelling" (p. 432), one best reserved to a religion class or Sunday School, as Kohn characterizes it.

The fourth rule of the grammar of Catholic schooling maintains that education is essentially a moral endeavor, an educational enterprise involved in the very hard work of translating a vision of what constitutes a truly good life into practical learning experiences that inculcate the values embedded in that vision of life into each student's experience. It is this moral vision that must be enacted in every classroom, by all teachers, so that each student has the maximum opportunity to learn how to act rightly and to avoid the deleterious consequences of those wrong choices that lead to a truly bad life. Anything short of a moral education is no education at all. Instead, it is mere skills training. In striking contrast to Kohn, who fears the possibility of religious indoctrination in public schools, Catholic educational philosophy maintains that the nation's citizenry should fear more any form of public schooling devoid of religious values.

Kohn is correct, however, in his assertion that Catholic schooling is essentially conservative in thrust. It strives to awaken in students an appreciation for the religious tradition from which they take their identity and to prepare them to make decisions about how they will live as they make the Catholic tradition incarnate, enacting their destiny as children of God. In 1917, T. J. Shahan, the President of the Catholic Educational Association (CEA), articulated this notion when told his audience gathered at the CEA's annual convention:

> ...[I]f early training in the schools prescinds from God and the divine order of life and the world; if the youthful mind be taught to recognize no holy and inviolable sanction of law, discipline and obedience; if the youthful heart learns to admire and love no ideals higher than those of materialism, hedonism, rationalism, then surely an era will set in of low, selfish, and mercenary convictions and the American State will one day come face to face with a general citizenship wedded to ignoble ease and comfort, disillusioned of the glorious Christian ideals on which it arose, and stubbornly averse to any sustained risks or exertions necessary to save them for posteriority. (p. 45)

The grammar of Catholic schooling shifts the focus of debate away from functional means to substantive ends. For Catholic educational philosophy, what is most useful to students is not what subjects students take while enrolled in school but the way a school's curriculum and instructional program foster an integral formation, that is, shaping beings who, as a result of the curriculum and instruction they receive throughout their years in school, will be rendered useful not only to themselves and to their society, but to their religion as well.

Ultimately, the fourth rule of the grammar of Catholic schooling maintains that the subject of education is the student not the subjects that students learn. While many concerned citizens might prefer to focus on the latter than the former, they are acting upon the invalid premise that students exist for schools. The grammar of Catholic schooling stands critical of this notion, asserting instead that schools exists for students.

Rule #5: Teaching is an intimate communication between souls.

The grammar of Catholic schooling confronts those 20th century educational theories and practices that deify pedagogical techniques over and above educational goals, that is, educational means before educational ends. This grammar does so by challenging the principles that lend support to the predominant technical-rational, means-end ideology restricting so much 20th century educational thought and practice. The grammar of Catholic schooling maintains that, while educational technology is important, it is only a secondary means to effect the

---

Identify the competencies of your teachers as classroom instructors, that is, what do they well:

_____
_____
_____
_____

Concerning teacher excellence, name two teachers and define one behavior that sets each apart from their colleagues:

Name: _____
Behavior: _____
_____
_____
_____

Name: _____
Behavior: _____
_____
_____
_____

At a faculty meeting and at a parents meeting discuss the vocation of the Catholic educator, using the anecdotal data you have gathered to draw attention to the presence of authentic Catholic teachers in your school.

> *Organize a series of in-service programs where your faculty is given time to reflect upon and to discuss the practical implications to their professional practice of:*
>
> - *the difference between instructing and educating youth;*
>
> - *the significance of forming a student's intellect and will; and,*
>
> - *educators as the symbolic presence of God active in the lives of their students.*

desired end, namely, the moral and intellectual formation of students.

At the same time, the grammar of Catholic schooling does not deny that expertise in teaching as well as the ability to utilize the most appropriate materials available are important tools in the pedagogical arsenal. Without doubt, it is incumbent upon all teachers to continuously hone their professional competence and specialized knowledge through years of study, experience and, in particular, reflection upon practice. In short, teachers must become expert in transmitting the knowledge, skills, and values associated with a sound educational program. Furthermore, teachers need assistance and encouragement as they confront the many personal and professional challenges that emerge each day within the confines of their classrooms. For, as veteran teachers know, what one plans to have transpire serves only as the architecture for what actually does occur. Classrooms are dynamic environments where teachers' plans and student lives intersect in oftentimes serendipitous ways. It is the master teacher who forges a purpose where all of these elements can coalesce in sound pedagogical practice.[6]

During a pontificate spanning 19 years, Pius XII (1939-1958) devoted portions of at least 106 encyclicals and speeches to educational themes. As this corpus relates to Catholic educational thought, it has served an important purpose: it clarifies and synthesizes 19th and 20th-century papal teaching concerning the education of youth and, in particular, the vocation and work of the Catholic educator (Jacobs, 1996). More importantly, the sheer volume of Pius XII's educational thought also concretizes the fifth rule of the grammar of Catholic schooling. That is, teaching excellence reveals itself best in the intimate communication transpiring between souls, namely, those of teachers and their students.

Pius XII uttered his clearest pronouncement concerning the teacher's vocation in his 1954 his radio message to the Fifth Inter-American Congress on Catholic Education meeting in Havana, Cuba. In this message, the Pope specified four characteristics of "good" teachers. It was his fourth characteristic that delineated the fifth rule of the grammar of Catholic schooling. The pontiff said:

> Good teachers, finally, are careful to educate rather than merely to instruct; they are capable, above all, of forming and of molding souls chiefly through contact with their own....To achieve this—We repeat—"be fathers of souls more than propagators of sterile information," form your pupils above all "by the example of your life." (1954b, pp 483-484)

In light of this ideal, the grammar of Catholic schooling maintains that teaching excellence involves much more than the timely and accurate transmission of information from a teacher, on the one hand, to a student or group of students, on the other. Teaching excellence is, in addition, the effective communication of a particular way of being human.

One year later, Pius XII spoke again regarding this ideal:

> "Teacher" is the highest title that can be given to an instructor. The teacher's function demands something higher and more profound than the function of the person who merely communicates a knowledge of things. The "teacher" is a person who knows how to create a close relationship between his own soul and the soul of a child. It is he who personally devotes himself to guiding the inexperienced pupil towards truth and virtue. It is he in a word, who molds the pupil's intellect and will so as to fashion as best he can a being of human and Christian perfection. (Pius XII, 1955, p. 514)

In light of this ideal, teaching is a privileged interaction relating a teacher with a student. It is a highly interactive relationship, motivated as much by the teacher's love of God and neighbor as it is the student's responsiveness to the teacher's revelation of God's love. It is through the intimate communication between two souls that teachers stimulate their students to see and to experience, through the teacher's words, acts, and affect, the incarnation of God's love active in the student's own life.

To achieve this effect in students, Pius XII argued, "[t]rue teachers must be complete persons and Christians...imitators of the only Divine Master Jesus Christ" (1955/1979, p. 514). These teachers must know their students by observing them. These teachers also talk with and listen to their students. Through these and other activities, teachers learn about their students and impress important things upon them, in particular, the wisdom of the Catholic faith that is absolutely indispensable to human existence.

In light of this ideal, if teachers are to fulfill what their vocation requires, the grammar of Catholic schooling maintains that teachers must not only know their students, but also must cooperate with God's grace. Teachers cannot expect their students to be perfect and to behave as mature, virtuous adults. That is, teachers must struggle patiently yet firmly with their students' shortcomings as they endeavor to root their students in virtue. As Lasley (1997) frames this notion:

> Values are caught, not taught. And once caught, they must be practiced. No short cuts to virtue exist....Our goal should be to become people of good character. That goal is achievable if we adults can see people as ends, not means; if we can see that people matter and need to be taken seriously and respected; and if we can see that we must be responsible as individuals for our own behavior (p. 655).

Obviously, good teachers do not merely instruct youth. More importantly, good teachers educate youth, drawing out of their students the virtuous self-disciplines required of them in order to participate as citizens not only of this world but of the next as well. Good teachers lead their students to become perfect, mature, and virtuous adults by modeling for their students a distinctive way of human life, for example, by challenging the mediocrity asserted by the peer group. In this and many other ways, these teachers set definable standards that have the potential to influence their students' entire adult lives in those decades ahead when their adolescent peer group has been left far behind. Through the privileged intimacy of the teacher-student relationship, good teachers guide their students to appreciate truths about nature, human existence, and God so that, as adults, they will be able to act upon these truths.

The vision of the teacher-student relationship conveyed by the fifth rule of grammar highlights the dynamic of Christian personalism that actuates authentic teaching and learning, from a Roman Catholic perspective. That is, as teachers imitate Jesus the Teacher, faith is not solely the dry, intellectual matter conveyed by the Catholic catechism and religion classes. Faith also defines how one will live one's life and use one's gifts and talents to further God's kingdom—for their students, the teacher's witness is God's living word incarnate in the teacher's pure, simple, humble, and generous deeds.

Christian personalism, exemplified by the intimate relationship between the souls of teacher and student, is what motivates students to grow morally and intellectually. Through their words and actions, teachers invite their students to participate in the life of a community that works together to learn important things. And, in schools where teachers and students speak with one another from their souls, moral virtues, like loyalty, courage, devotion to duty, as well as love of family and country are inspired, practiced, and inculcated. Even in inner-city schools, where students experience their teachers caring for them as unique, special, and talented human beings, these students desire to learn things in school and to remain in schools, (Bryk, Lee, & Holland, 1993) not merely because schooling is a legal requirement or a means to achieve some modicum of worldly success.

Thus, Catholic educational philosophy asserts that educating youth is not merely a profession, one of many job opportunities available to women and men. Rather, Catholic educational philosophy argues that devoting one's life to educate youth is a vocation, a call from God to each teacher's heart, stirring those generous women and men to devote their talents and energies to make youth "the architects of the social restoration in Christ" (Pius XII, 1945, p. 342). In Pius XII's words,

> There are thousands of adolescents entrusted to you during the delicate years of their development; you have a serious responsibility for the formation of...youth and you are making an important contribution to the preparation of a better future for your country. As Christians, you cannot remain indifferent, as teachers, you have the joy of being able

to cooperate effectively in the renewal of your generation. (Pius XII, 1954b, p. 481)

The fifth rule of the grammar of Catholic education identifies precisely what it is that motivates students. Competent instruction provides the basis for humans to exchange and to understand important knowledge. This evidences itself in the significant outcomes attested to by the research into Catholic school effectiveness (Bryk *et al.*, 1993; Coleman & Hoffer, 1982; Coleman *et al.*, 1987). But, more significantly, it is the intimate conversation between the teachers, their students, and the pedagogical relationship characterized by Christian personalism, which enflames the restless desire of youth to imitate the heroic sanctity of Jesus the Teacher, the Risen Lord embodied in their teachers. Were parents to believe that the whole of a child's life feeds upon the effects of these elementary and secondary teachers, there probably would exist in the United States a very different conception of educational accountability. One thing is for sure, as Sergiovanni and Starratt (1988) have noted, teachers' contracts would be replaced with educational covenants binding parents and educators together in the joint venture called schooling.

Rule #6: Educational decisions are best made locally.

Surveying the terrain of schooling in the United States, especially during the middle and closing decades of the 20th century, it would be a rather difficult assignment to find a public school system that did not exhibit a hierarchical organizational structure which included an elected Board of Education, a Superintendent, at least several Assistant (and/or Associate) Superintendents, numerous specialists (e.g., Curriculum, Special Education, Governmental Affairs), and multiple building principals. It would be an equally daunting venture to find a public school whose organizational structure did not mime the larger system's prevailing structure. In the prototypical public school, several administrative layers report to the building principal, with teachers frequently reporting to intermediaries, for example, assistant principals or program (or department) directors, rather than reporting directly to the principal.

Viewing this now-traditional organizational structure through the historical lens provided by Tyack and Tobin's (1994) grammar of public schooling, what is of consequence for thinking about Catholic schooling is the organization of how the industrial model has and continues to monopolize practically all schooling. And, what is of far greater significance is the hegemony this model exercises, so much so that any challenge to the dominant organizational design is regarded as tantamount to sedition. Indeed, it is the cult of efficiency that has ruled this era (Callahan, 1962), defining the orthodox way of conducting business, educationally speaking.

As teaching in a Catholic school relates to instructing youth, your teachers fulfill an important function. Identify three outcomes associated with instructional competence:
1)_____
2)_____
3)_____

As teaching in a Catholic school relates to educating youth, your teachers fulfill a significant moral role. Identify three outcomes associated with pedagogical excellence:
1)_____
2)_____
3)_____

In your role as principal, how might you work to foster the development of these outcomes? What skills do you need to be effective in achieving this goal? Where might you go to receive this training?

> **Take a few moments to reflect upon the governance structure of your school**:
>
> - Does it reflect the prevailing industrial model with its impersonal bureaucratic layers and policies?
>
> - When your teachers complain about their work, how do you deal with their frustrations (e.g., privately with an individual, collectively with the group, not at all)?
>
> - Identify the educational expert in your school.
>
> - What do your honest responses to these questions suggest about how your envision your leadership role? It is oriented more toward functional management or substantive leadership?

Probing into the orthodox design a bit, the locus of decision-making is quite explicit: decisions emanate from role incumbents whose jobs are positioned at the top of the organizational chart (the "head," *capitus* in Latin, those men—for the most part—whose hierarchical roles encase the "organizational brains"). Decisions emanating from the head of this vertical hierarchy are implemented by individuals whose jobs are located somewhere below the top of the chart (the organizational "hand," *manus* in Latin, those women—for the most part—who are the organization's "manual laborers"). For the nation's public schools, in particular, this model defines the reality of work, where teachers, as interchangeable organizational inferiors, are paid to enact decisions made by their hierarchical superiors. Little interactive communication is needed between hierarchical levels—or perhaps even desired. That is, teachers are interchangeable organizational functionaries who do what they are contracted to do and to get their job done in the most efficient way possible.

For better or for worse, even Catholic schooling has imitated the predominant organizational model, all in an effort to demonstrate that Catholic schools are every bit as good as their public school counterparts. All the while, however, the Church's social teaching criticized this organizational model, particularly as industry deified it in the late 19th century. Invoking the philosophical principle of subsidiarity as its standard of judgment, the Church upheld the keystones of vibrant community life, namely, the dignity, contributions, and challenges that individuals offer a community as well as the importance of the transcendent value of community itself and the challenges which the transcendent value of community provides its members.

For the Church, the foremost exemplar of this model of social organization is the nuclear family.

In this tiny community, each individual possesses an unqualified and unique dignity and purpose which, as this dignity and purpose is brought to fulfillment, contributes to the family in such a way that the richness of family life increases. To be more specific, both father and mother contribute in different yet complimentary ways to the richness of family life. Children, too, make their own contribution, as only children can. Aunts, uncles, grandparents, and in some instances, even close family friends, make significant contributions to family life by sacrificing themselves to partake of and to promote a shared purpose. Thus, by taking initiative and contributing to family life, each individual makes it possible for others to experience the joy of participating in a community of people who love, cherish, and value each other. And, as each individual flourishes within the community of the nuclear family, so too, the family flourishes.

Notice how this quality of richness is noticeably absent when, for example, a family member is absent or rendered incapable of functioning (e.g., in situations of illness). In the instance when some exigency (e.g., illness) makes it difficult, if not impossible, for a family member to contribute to family life, other members of the family (and, in this sense, the family unit itself) share in the obligation to offer assistance until that person is once again capable of contributing to the family. However, this selfless generosity is not an unlimited resource. Assistance is lovingly offered with the intention that the individual will once again take initiative when capable of contributing to the family. Except in rare or rather tragic circumstances, people do not offer assistance with the understanding that the individual will become dependent on the family or its members, a situation that is not good, either for the individual or the family.

So too, subsidiarity upholds the dignity of the individual and the contributions that individuals make to the life of the larger community. Like a family, no community can function effectively if its members do not contribute to the common good or if the community does not band together to provide assistance for its members who are in need.

Thus, subsidiarity requires women and men to strike a balance, a very delicate balance achieved only as individuals contribute to the community's life and as the community provides for itself and its members' needs, without stifling individual initiative, on the one hand, or restraining individual autonomy unduly, on the other hand. In those instances when individuals and communities are not able to provide for their needs, subsidiarity tolerates only the minimal amount of external intervention necessary to restore the community to its former health.

The principle of subsidiarity...

The ideal enshrined in the principle of subsidiarity locates initiative and responsibility at the smallest unit of social organization, namely, the individual, whether the organization is the family, a neighborhood or town, or the nation. Individual initiative courses its stream upwards, not downwards, as each individual utilizes his or her gifts and talents in such ways that enrich the community of the family, neighborhood or town, or the nation. And, at different times and based upon differing individual needs, the community of the family, neighborhood or town, or the nation must promote, restrain, or assist individuals so that the common good will thrive.

Pius XI framed the philosophical ideal animating this image of community in his 1931 encyclical, *Quadragesimo anno*:

> It is indeed true, as history clearly shows, that owing to the change in social conditions, much that was formerly done by small bodies can nowadays be accomplished only by large organizations. Nevertheless, it is a fundamental principle of social philosophy, *fixed and unchangeable*, that one should not withdraw from individuals and commit to the community what they can accomplish by their own enterprise and

The Grammar of Catholic Schooling

industry. So, too, it is an injustice and at the same time a grave evil and a disturbance of right order to transfer to the larger and higher collectivity functions which can be performed and provided for by lesser and subordinate bodies. Inasmuch as every social activity should, by its very nature, prove a help to members of the body social, it should never destroy or absorb them. (1931, #79, italics added)

Quadragesimo anno took dead-aim at two social problems emerging as the Industrial Revolution impacted communities. The first problem concerned the negative impact industrialization had upon human beings, particularly the commodification and depersonalization of work as well as the forfeiture of basic human rights and responsibilities to large, industrial organizations. In response to these social problems, *Quadragesimo anno* raised two fundamental questions: Is human work solely consequence of sin, to be endured until retirement or death? And: If work is more than this, how is it to be organized to promote a good quality of life for communities and their members?

The second social problem *Quadragesimo anno* raised concerned how society would balance individual initiative and promote the common good with only the minimum of governmental intervention. The Industrial Revolution made it more difficult to achieve this delicate balance especially as the more personal and subjective type of human relationships predominating pre-industrial, rural-agrarian communities were eclipsed by the more impersonal and objective type of relationships necessitated by urban-industrial society (Toënnies, 1964). This careful balance was further upset by the rise of nationalism which envisioned the individual not as a unique and distinctive human person but as a citizen possessing a distinct nationality and allegiance. At the heart of the second problem was a profound question concerning social responsibility: Without a vibrant community comprised of strong personal relationships, what were individuals, communities, and national governments to do for the downtrodden, especially when these women and men can no longer cope in a society best suited to the survival of the fittest?

Reflecting upon these social problems, Pius XI elaborated the principle of subsidiarity, maintaining that governmental authorities "should leave to other bodies the care and expediting of business and activities of lesser moment....It then will perform with greater freedom, vigor and effectiveness, the tasks belonging properly to it, and which it alone can accomplish, directing, supervising, encouraging, restraining, as circumstances suggest or necessity demands" (1931, #80).

Pius XI's communitarian ideal shifted the burden of primary responsibility for intervening in situations of genuine human need away from a central government and to the individual members of local communities. These individuals, Pius XI reasoned, were not only in the best position to be aware of, but also to provide for their fellow citizens' needs. For example, providing food for the hungry and shelter for the

---

Think about the metaphor, "the school as a learning community."

- Identify individual members of your faculty who promote the common good.

- Cite instances when you have challenged members of your school community to become less self-interested and to promote the common good.

- Name the one individual in your school who best exemplifies the communitarian ideal, one who sacrifices self-interest in order to promote the common good.

- As part of your school's Teacher Appreciation Day festivities, tell your school community a story about this individual who teaches these values as they are embodied in someone they know, respect, and love.

homeless might immediately come to mind as examples of this ideal being translated into concrete action. However, the lives and pious works of those 19th century women and men who banded together in religious communities and dedicated themselves to providing, among other things, education for immigrant Catholic youth, health care for the sick and infirmed, as well as orphanages for homeless and abandoned children best exemplify the communitarian perspective articulated by Pius XI. In theory, at least, the proper role of government is to assist these groups by "directing, supervising, encouraging, restraining, as circumstances suggest or necessity demands," in order that "a hierarchical order prevails among the various organizations, [and] the more excellent will be the authority and efficiency of society..." (#80).

And yet, even as the Industrial Revolution redefined human labor, women and men in an ever-increasing number of workplaces, including schools, discovered themselves reduced to the role of an organizational "drone" (Jackall, 1988) enslaved in an organizational "iron cage" (Weber, 1930). The dire social consequences of this aspect of industrialization, as well as those resulting from the trend toward urbanization and the tidal wave of immigration, soon became evident in the United States, at least, in rising rates of alcoholism, the breakdown of the family, and increased juvenile delinquency. Social problems like these led Pius XI to press social reformers, the would-be architects of utopian societies, to resolve these problems. Pius XI inquired: What is a community to do when its pious societies are so overwhelmed that they cannot provide for the truly destitute? Was the community to abandon the needy and leave them to fend for themselves?

The communitarian ideal Pius XI defined in *Quadragesimo anno* did not absolve government of its responsibility to intervene in the plight of the destitute. Instead, he reasoned, the proper exercise of government necessitates a form of intervention synonymous with providing assistance, that is, government exercises its authority best at the macro-level by providing the help needed for local communities to meet their members' needs, at the micro-level. At the same time, the Pius XI maintained, in the extreme case where this ideal could not be realized, direct government intervention into the life of the community would be necessary, but only until the community could provide for its members' needs on its own.

What Pius XI argued for was governmental *assistance* for the truly needy, not a massive infusion of government into the lives of individuals or communities. He viewed the latter as an unacceptable form of governmental intrusion that ultimately would displace individual initiative and community responsibility for human beings with an extensive and, in some cases, permanent governmental bureaucracy that would be more responsive to its own interests than to the plight of the truly needy. Therefore, *Quadragesimo anno* asserted that governmental in-

---

If your teachers experienced themselves as drones imprisoned in an iron cage, list what you as school leader would be called to do on behalf of your faculty:

1)_____

2)_____

3)_____

The Grammar of Catholic Schooling

When a school functions as a learning community, what values, attitudes, and skills must characterize the principal?

values:
_____
_____
_____

attitudes:
_____
_____
_____

skills:
_____
_____
_____

What leadership skills are required if these values, attitudes, and skills are to course upward through the school rather than downward through the formal hierarchy?

tervention was to be just that—assistance for citizens who could not provide for themselves and whose community did not have resources sufficient to the need. One practical application of this abstract ideal is found in the United States in those instances when the Federal Emergency Management Agency (FEMA) directly intervenes in communities beset by natural disasters. FEMA provides direct assistance and coordinates overall recovery efforts by providing temporary shelter, medical attention, and the reconstruction of basic infrastructure until the community is once again able to care for itself and its members.

Pope John Paul II elaborated upon his predecessors' model in his 1991 encyclical, *Centesimus annus*. Having experienced first-hand the difficulties of life in a communist state and its debilitating impact upon people and their communities, John Paul II reiterated the importance of balancing individual initiative, community responsibility, and governmental intervention. In *Centesimus annus*, John Paul II argued that subsidiarity evidences itself when "a community of a higher order [does] not interfere in the internal life of a community of a lower order, depriving the latter of its functions, but rather [does] support it in case of need and help to coordinate its activity with the activities of the rest of society, always with a view to the common good" (48.100).

John Paul II grounded his explication of subsidiarity in an ecclesiological vision where the Church contributes to the political order not through its support for or critique of political systems *per se* but rather, by upholding "the dignity of the person revealed in all its fullness in the mystery of the Incarnate Word" (47.99). For the Church, the Incarnation is the absolute standard by which the Church evaluates actions by nation-states and their agents. For example, in *Centesimus annus* John Paul II directly criticizes the "welfare state" (and, by another name, "the social assistance state"), arguing that the malfunctions and defects of the welfare state are a direct consequence of an inadequate understanding of the Incarnation which, in turn, allows states to exercise their proper tasks improperly. He argues:

> By intervening directly and depriving society of its responsibility, the Social Assistance State leads to a loss of human energies and an inordinate increase of public agencies, which are dominated more by bureaucratic ways of thinking than by concern for serving their clients, and which are accompanied by an enormous increase in spending. In fact, it would appear that needs are best understood and satisfied by people who are closest to them and who act as neighbors to those in need. (49.101)

For the Church, what is at issue is not what political system nurtures and supports the welfare state, but whether or not an individual human being's genuine needs are being adequately provided for by people who are near to and able to express their heartfelt care. An impersonal, functional, and bureaucratic response, even though it might provide for a case of genuine need, is simply not sufficient to provide for genuine *human* needs. No state bureaucracy can replace the members of a community, who express their care by watching out for one another and by providing for their needs.

Thus, Pope John Paul II directs the Church's criticism not at any political system (e.g., Marxist socialism or American capitalism) but at how these political systems impact individual human beings, especially the poor. In particular, John Paul II argues that the social dimensions of subsidiarity require governments and their agents to make decisions cognizant of and responsive to authentic human needs rather than for political, organizational, or administrative ends (which oftentimes seek only to preserve and extend themselves as well as to deplete limited financial resources for administrative and operational expenses rather than for human needs). Given this context for decision-making, John Paul II maintains that any governmental intervention in the life of a local community "must be as brief as possible, so as to avoid removing permanently from society and business systems the functions which are properly theirs, and so as to avoid enlarging excessively the sphere of state intervention to the detriment of both economic and civil freedom" (48.99). Thus, in theory, at least, the Church respects diverse political systems as well as the right of legitimate governmental authority to make decisions about what must be done to meet the needs of local communities and their members.

In sum, when the Church criticizes governmental intervention into the life of a community and its members, what is at issue is not the political system *per se* but whether the model of social organization engendered by the political system is providing assistance to the local community to provide for its members' genuine needs. Negatively put, subsidiarity makes it possible for the Church to stand critical of any form of social organization that endeavors to further its own interests by making communities dependent upon that organization as the sole provider of what the community needs. As a consequence of this reasoning, subsidiarity does not provide a government a road map specifying what that government must do in those instances where an genuine need has been identified. Instead, subsidiarity challenges those women and men who bear the mantle of governance to exercise imagination and creativity in determining just how the government will provide for the needs of local communities while, at the same time, not intervening in ways that stifle individual initiative and responsibility for fostering the common good as well as denigrate the community's responsibility to provide for its members needs.

Even though the nation's Catholic bishops wrote their 1986 pastoral letter *Economic Justice for All* prior to John Paul II's issuance of *Centesimus annus*, the bishops asserted a similar notion as they revisited the principle of subsidiarity. Reinvoking Pius XI's communitarian ideal to define the proper relationship between individual initiative, community responsibility, and governmental intervention, the bishops wrote:

> [The principle of subsidiarity] states that, in order to protect basic justice, government should undertake only those initiatives which exceed the capacity of individuals or private groups smaller communities and individual acting independently. Government should not replace or destroy initiative. Rather it should help them to contribute more effectively to social well-being and supplement their activity when the demands of justice exceed their capacities. This does not mean, however, that the government that governs least governs best. Rather it defines good government intervention as that which truly "helps" other social groups contribute to the common good by directing, urging, restraining, and regulating economic activity as the occasion requires and necessity demands. This calls for cooperation and consensus-building among the diverse agents in our economic life, including government. The precise form of government involvement in this process cannot be determined in the abstract. It will depend on an assessment of specific needs and the most effective ways to address them. (National Conference of Catholic Bishops, 1986, #124)

The American bishops' 1986 pastoral letter negates any harsh or extreme applications of the principle of subsidiarity. For example, a political party must stand critical of any individual, group, or organization that would deny government the right to intervene directly in the plight (for example, of needy urban children) arguing that the individual, group, or organization should leave these children and their families to fend for themselves in the arduous struggle for survival. At the same time, *Economic Justice for All* supports those political platforms asserting that it is not the proper role of government to intervene (for example, in urban affairs) in any way that threatens to destroy individual initiative or lessen the community's responsibility to provide for its citizens' needs.

In sum, the principle of subsidiary charges those who govern to be creative as they strike a rather delicate balance between what is in each individual's as well as in each community's self-interest. The support structures sustaining healthy communities thrive (namely, individual initiative and responsibility for the common good as well as the community's responsibility to provide for its members needs) while governmental intervention is kept to a minimum when this balance is achieved.

Subsidiarity and Catholic educational leadership practice...

As an abstract concept, the principle of subsidiarity might seem unrelated to the very practical, day-to-day realities Catholic educational leaders confront. However, this abstract theory has very practical implications, offering a rich philosophical context for thinking about many of the contentious issues involved in educating youth, especially as these issues encumber parents, the Church, and the state. Furthermore, in its application, subsidiarity provides a framework for Catholic educational leaders to examine, to prod, and to challenge their own thought, as well as that of their fellow citizens, concerning how parents, local communities, and the state and federal governments might interact in the very important societal issue about how best to provide for the moral and intellectual formation of youth.

The philosophical ideal of subsidiarity offers a dramatic contrast to the predominant industrial model of organizational decision-making introduced earlier, the model that has characterized American schooling for much of the 20th century. For example, after several generations, many citizens are now accustomed to the fact that educational decisions are made by bureaucrats in state capitols and in the nation's capital—far removed from the reality of schools, classrooms, and especially, teachers and their students. Taxpayers expect these elected or appointed bureaucrats to enact decisions, oftentimes dictating to citizens what they are to do about educating children, whether these people are parents, school board members, superintendents and principals, or teachers and their students. When it comes to schooling, impersonal policies, rules, and regulations—the hallmark of a 20th century industrial organization—have superseded personal initiative, the struggle to identify and define genuine human needs, as well as the very necessary and hard work of consensus-building within a democratic community—all of which serve to solidify and enhance community life. As the experience of the 20th century points out, when impersonal policies, rules, and regulations define schooling, schools themselves quickly become institutions that provide youth prescribed instruction in required subjects. And yet, even when these institutions do provide youth an adequate intellectual formation, these schools have actually failed youth, if only because these institutions have not provided a moral formation, that is, inculcating in young women and men the refined ability that will render them capable of sacrificing themselves and their self-interest to be of service to their community, nation, and religion in the next generation when the mantle of authority descends upon their shoulders.

As subsidiarity concerns Catholic schools, the decentralized organizational ideal stands in contrast to the model of organization adopted but never fully implemented by the nation's dioceses during the 20th century. As standardization slowly infected the organization of American public schooling in the first three decades of the 20th century, so too the Church's new code of canon law (1919), the gradual expansion of chancery offices and departments, as well as the press to meet state-

Compare and contrast these three images:
- *your school as an "organization."*
- *your school as an "institution," and,*
- *your school as a "community."*

Describe the implications you perceive each image having for:
- *the principal's job description;*
- *the role and function of the teacher;*
- *parental involvement;*
- *the role of pastors; and,*
- *the purpose of the diocesan schools office.*

mandated accreditation standards could have interacted in ways that usurped the highly decentralized organizational structure of U.S. Catholic schooling (Dolan, 1985; Jacobs, 1997a). But, even with increased diocesan centralization as well as the emergence of national educational groups, like the NCEA and the National Catholic Welfare Conference (now called the United States Catholic Conference, or simply "USCC") Department of Education, U.S. Catholic schooling has remained largely decentralized, for better or worse (Bryk *et al.*, 1993; McCarren, 1966).

This outcome certainly has been for the better for Catholic schooling, if only for the reason that Catholic schooling derives its mandate from the philosophical premise that parents are the primary educators of their children. It is this premise (what is the third rule of the grammar of Catholic schooling) that succinctly expresses the fundamental organizing principle of Catholic schooling, namely, parents determine how their children will receive the moral and intellectual formation they need to become fully-functioning, adult citizens. Only then should the religious and civic communities intervene in the sometimes contentious and more oftentimes than not political struggle to balance parental self-interest and initiative.

Subsidiarity challenges parents, in their role as Catholic educational leaders, to take seriously their obligation to provide for the moral and intellectual formation of their children. Because this obligation comes from God, parents are not free to abdicate the education of their children to nameless and faceless governmental bureaucrats in locales far-removed. Instead, parents must work with their neighbors as well as the larger civic community to insure that their daughters and sons receive the educational program their parents desire. And, in those instances where the community cannot provide resources adequate to the need, subsidiarity reminds parents that the community of the Church and the civil government, too, are ready to provide the assistance parents need so that their children will receive the moral and intellectual formation that parents want and which promotes the common good.

In the United States, where a strict wall of separation has been drawn between Church and State, the parish community serves as the focal point where Catholic parents may reflect upon and make decisions regarding their obligation to provide for the educational needs of their children. For nearly 200 years in the United States, many Catholic parents have turned to the community of the local parish to find a source of support and encouragement as they have struggled to provide for the educational needs of their daughters and sons. For generations, the abstract concept of subsidiarity has had real implications for pastors, challenging them to fulfill their pastoral obligation to see to it that every Catholic child receives the very best moral formation possible. Many pastors have responded generously to this challenge, devoting their time and efforts to provide for the educational needs of Catholic youth, if only for the somewhat parochial reason that these youngsters will become the next generation's Catholic leaders. So too, parish boards of education have shared in this pastoral obligation over the generations by studying the issues associated with subsidizing a program of moral formation for youth (and frequently, an intellectual formation as well), concluding that they must invite their fellow parishioners to commit themselves and limited parish resources to this important endeavor.

Unfortunately, however, for all too long the debate regarding Catholic education has devolved to the bottom lines of balance sheets and income statements rather than a careful consideration of moral imperatives. However, close scrutiny of research comparing the number of years students spend in Catholic schools and their practice of the faith as adults (Greeley, 1989), places before Catholic educational leaders the inevitable conclusion that the imperative to provide youth a moral and intellectual formation is not simply financial. For, in the long run, any generation's failure to respond to its obligation to provide youth the very best program not only of intellectual but, more importantly, of moral formation is a failure of leadership that could debilitate the Church in the next generation. Without doubt, any failure to evangelize youth in the faith and practice of the Church in this generation will become evident in the next generation when Catholic adults neither appreciate nor act upon their moral responsibilities.

Subsidiarity also offers practical challenges to diocesan officials, reminding them of their obligation to address the educational needs confronting parishes. While it may be fashionable to make pronouncements about the Church's solidarity with and preferential option for the poor, subsidiarity challenges diocesan authorities to exercise educational leadership by standing in solidarity with the morally impoverished, especially those children whose parents, pastors, parish boards of education, and pastors are incapable of providing for the educational needs of children. For diocesan officials, subsidiarity puts the matter in proper perspective: these officials and their agencies are obliged to intervene in local parish communities by providing the assistance which these communities require, if they are to provide for their youngest members' genuine needs, especially their need for a program of moral formation.

Turning our focus to Catholic schools, subsidiarity implies many things, especially for the women and men working in them. First of all, subsidiarity implies that educators in Catholic schools must be vigilant in upholding the primacy of parental rights. When confronted by angry or upset parents, subsidiarity reminds educators in Catholic schools that they cannot blame nameless and faceless bureaucrats for why things are the way they are. Instead, these educators must carefully balance Church teaching, diocesan (and perhaps parish) policies, and professional standards with parental rights. While subsidiarity does not provide any easy answers to these troublesome and sometimes awkward situations,

When subsidiarity is defined as providing "needed assistance," define what principals must do for:

youth: _____
_____
_____

teachers: _____
_____
_____

parents: _____
_____
_____

subsidiarity does provide norms to inform decision-making and, by so doing, upholds the dignity of the teachers and principals who have devoted their lives to serving in Catholic schools on behalf of parents.

Furthermore, subsidiarity provides a framework to understand the legitimate exercise of authority in Catholic schools. In general, subsidiarity recognizes as primary the individual's responsibility to promote the common good. It is this communitarian norm which takes precedence to individual rights and selfish self-interest. In light of this decision-making *a priori,* parents, pastors, parish boards of education, and educators in Catholic schools exercise their educational leadership by seeking to empower all members of the school community to promote the school's Catholic identity. This is the clear, shared, common purpose for which each of these individuals exercise their authority (Jacobs 1997b).

Consequently, subsidiarity provides a normative framework for thinking about how Catholic schooling can be organized and how, on the one hand, parents, pastors, parish boards of education as well as principals and teachers in Catholic schools exercise their leadership. For example, subsidiarity reminds parents and pastors that they are not educational experts—possessing an all-encompassing knowledge of what constitutes best educational practice. Parents, as the primary educators of their children, and pastors, as the *pater familias*—the father of the parish community—possess a legitimate interest and obligation to see to it that each child in the parish receives the very best possible program of moral and intellectual formation. And, in order to achieve this goal, parents, pastors, and parish boards of education invite professional educators to stand *in loco parents* by providing for the educational needs of their children. Thus, subsidiarity reminds parents, pastors, and parish boards of education that educators in Catholic schools are not hired employees. Instead, they are Jesus' disciples. They have been invited to assist pastors and parishes in furthering the moral and intellectual formation of the youth that parents and the parish community entrust to their ministry.

On the other hand, subsidiarity reminds principals that they are not dictators—hired to tell teachers, students, parents, or pastors what they are to do. Instead, subsidiarity specifies the principal's proper exercise of authority as that of service, namely, providing assistance to parents and teachers so that they might provide for the educational needs of youth. Subsidiarity also reminds principals that teachers are not functionaries—replaceable cogs in the machinery of Catholic schooling. Teachers in Catholic schools are professionals, yes. More importantly, however, they are Jesus' disciples, women and men who devote themselves each day to forming youth, morally and intellectually. Thus, every teacher in a Catholic school is a precious resource. Each day, these women and men come to the Catholic school endeavoring to be Christ's

---

The local parish is the religious community where parents can reflect upon and seek assistance in providing for the educational needs of their children.

Identify three ways your parish can provide this forum for parents:
1)_____
2)_____
3)_____

living presence in their students' lives. Principals are leaders, forging an educational covenant with their teachers. But, principals must first reverence their teachers for responding to their vocation to teach as Jesus did.

In light of these challenges, subsidiarity constitutes three goals for Catholic schooling. First: *parents must be involved in the school as must pastors and the members of the parish board of education.*

For parents, providing for the moral and intellectual formation of their children is not simply a matter of paying tuition and dropping their children off at school around 7:45 a.m., and then returning to school around 3:15 p.m. to pick them up—or, worse yet, leaving their children to fend for themselves at school, home, or in the neighborhood until their parents arrive home after 5:00 p.m. Subsidiarity demands much more of parents. They must work in concert with the principal and teachers to bring the school's purposes to fruition if only because educators stand *in loco parentis*. Also, parents must know, understand, and support the school's educational programs and curricular goals. It is not enough for parents to assume that what transpires in the Catholic school meets their expectations. Parents must also endeavor to insure that what takes place in school extends the educational lessons that parents are providing in the home. Conversely, parents must be careful not to contradict or minimize the moral and intellectual lessons their children are being taught in school. Lastly, parents must be actively involved in the events built into the school calendar. Active participation not only demonstrates to children that their parents care for and are interested in them; active parental involvement fosters a climate that enhances the school's ability to build social capital in its students (Coleman, 1987a, 1987b, 1988, 1991). Consequently, subsidiarity reminds parents that, when they send their children to a Catholic school, they are not contracting a professional service for a set (or negotiated) fee. Rather, parents delegate educators in Catholic schools to provide youth the moral and intellectual educational experiences their parents desire and practice within the confines of the domestic Church, that is, the home. Sending children to Catholic schools does not absolve parents of their responsibility to remain involved in the education of their children. Quite the contrary, subsidiarity requires greater, more meaningful, and more authentic involvement in the school's programs.

Second: *principals and teachers form a community of educators.* That is, principals are in Catholic schools not to dictate what teachers must do in their classrooms; instead, principals serve teachers by providing the assistance teachers need to translate the school's goals into learning experiences. Further, principals cannot work in isolation from classrooms nor can teachers distance themselves from administrative realities. In the Catholic school, principals and teachers share educational leadership and the administrative responsibilities associated with

---

Subsidiarity asserts that decisions are made with a view to the common good. Assess the decision-making process in your school:

- *Are decisions made only after gathering the relevant facts or giving first consideration to the school's mission?*

- *Are decisions made by the community of educators or by individuals who fill organizational roles?*

- *How are decisions justified? Does the rationale represent an impersonal bureaucratic orientation or an ethic of care that upholds the dignity of the individual as well as the school's mission?*

In light of the theory of subsidiarity, identify three challenges to your school's decision-making process:
1)_____
2)_____
3)_____

The Grammar of Catholic Schooling

> *As an individual who exercises governance in a Catholic school community:*
>
> - *Conceptualize your work in terms of encouraging individual initiative while upholding the community's responsibility for each of its members.*
>
> - *Envision a model of cooperative governance and consensus-building that would work in your school.*
>
> - *Specify the concrete needs of your students and teachers.*
>
> - *Identify strategies that will help you to assist your teachers learn how they can contribute to and further to the common good.*
>
> *Using this information, define your Catholic educational leadership agenda:*

it. Catholic schools characterized by subsidiarity will evidence principals and teachers who form a community focused primarily upon their school's purpose and how they assist one another for the benefit of their students.

For pastors, subsidiarity suggests that providing youth a moral and intellectual formation is not simply a matter of hiring a principal to administer the school, of paying the bills incurred, writing a check for the high school assessment, or offering a weekly (or monthly) all-school Mass. Pastors are required to be intimately involved in the complete schooling experience, including being present in the school building, cafeteria, library, and the school yard. For example, teaching religion class is an excellent way pastors can provide a moral formation for youth. In those instances where a central high school serves several parishes, it is incumbent upon pastors to be visibly present to their young parishioners. Having lunch and visiting with the students in the school cafeteria, celebrating (or concelebrating) mass for them, or even inviting them to the rectory for a cookout are ways that pastors can exhibit Catholic educational leadership and participate more meaningfully in the moral formation of the youth God has entrusted to their ministry.

Third: subsidiarity challenges organizations like diocesan educational offices that *their purpose is to assist parents and local parishes to provide for the moral formation of Catholic youth.* Diocesan offices cannot be content to produce policies and reams of procedural guidelines expecting that, as educators implement these, schools will become more Catholic. In place of thick policy books and bureaucratic regulations, diocesan schools offices must offer parents, pastors, parish boards of education, dioceses, principals, and teachers resources that will assist them to provide youth the very best moral formation.

In sum, subsidiarity challenges all of these individuals and groups to become involved and to collaborate with one another in achieving the shared goal of providing Catholic youth the very best formation available.

Involvement, however, does not connote *interference*.

For their part, parents need to allow educators to perform their professional obligations unencumbered by undue parental concern and anxiety about what is going on in the school. Although it is oftentimes a difficult challenge, parents must recall that they have entrusted their children to those educators and should be willing to accord them the professional deference this sacred covenant deserves. It is a very delicate balance, indeed.

For pastors and parish school boards, subsidiarity implies much the same as it does for bishops and diocesan educational officials. Even though pastors and school boards are in closer proximity to the school than diocesan officials, both jointly share the responsibility to insure that the local Catholic school is faithful to its purpose and actively translates

> *Identify three programs that involve parents in your school:*
> 1) _____
> 2) _____
> 3) _____
>
> *How might parental involvement be expanded to involve parents more meaningfully in your school's curricular and extra-curricular programs?*

Church teaching, diocesan educational policy directives, as well as local contingencies into concrete educational experiences. Because the role of pastor and school board member affords these individuals greater proximity to the school, these members of the community know in more elaborate and intimate detail what is transpiring in the local Catholic school. But, this knowledge does not give them the right to interfere in the daily operations of the Catholic school.

Principals, for their part, must know what is going on in the classrooms throughout the school building. However, this does not mean that principals should "snoopervise," lurking around the school in the vain attempt to know what is going on at every moment of every day. After all, principals should remember, teachers are present in classrooms to provide desired educational services. For the most part, teachers in Catholic schools provide those services quite well. In those instances where this is not happening, principals need to provide teachers the necessary assistance that will remediate any lack.

In sum, subsidiarity provides a supportive philosophical framework for the sixth rule of the grammar of Catholic schooling, a rule asserting that the best educational decisions are those made locally, first by parents—in the privacy of their homes, the "domestic church"—and then by local school boards—in the public forum where individuals and groups debate and define how the common good will be provided for. It is only in those (hopefully rare and unfortunate) circumstances when parents and local communities cannot provide for the educational needs of youth, that government intervention becomes necessary. But, it must not be forgotten, subsidiarity limits the degree to which external entities, like the Church and government, may intervene in the life of the community. Subsidiarity restricts intervention to providing necessary assistance, in this case, helping parents and communities to provide for the educational needs of their children. This philosophical concept does not allow either the Church or the government to replace individual initiative and responsibility or the community's responsibility for its members.

Summary: The grammar of Catholic schooling...

This chapter has detailed six normative rules forming the "grammar of Catholic schooling." As with the grammar of any language system, this grammar was not created *ex nihilo*. Nor was it designed by an omniscient power elite and imposed upon schools by layers of impersonal bureaucrats. Neither was the grammar of Catholic schooling shaped in response to the latest and most popular educational trends, fads, or gimmicks.

Instead, the grammar of Catholic schooling represents the wisdom of the Catholic community, a collective wisdom honed across centuries of experience as the Church and its members have fulfilled

---

As an abstract concept, subsidiarity requires close collaboration between all Catholic educational leaders.

Cite how you might engage each of the following in meaningful school governance:

parents: _____
_____
_____

pastors: _____
_____
_____

board members: _____
_____
_____

teachers: _____
_____
_____

students: _____
_____
_____

Jesus' mandate to "teach all nations" (Mark 16:15), albeit in very different times and places. It is the grammar of Catholic schooling, then, that represents Catholic educational "tradition," in Pelikan's (1971) sense of the term, that is, a grammar representing "the living faith of the dead" (p. 9). This grammar provides a schematic outline offering insight into the substantive core animating what is done in Catholic schools while its rules express why educators in Catholic schools do what they do in Catholic schools but with differing moral and intellectual outcomes than those of their peers in the nation's public schools.

Those who oppose Catholic schooling oftentimes portray it and the rules of its grammar as static or "traditional," as Pelkian (1971) would define that term. To these contrarians, Catholic schooling represents "the dead faith of the living" (p. 9). If this contrarian view accurately depicts the reality, the Catholic community in this generation would merely replicate what Catholics have done in previous generations as they went about resolving the very difficult and complex issues and challenges inherent when parents and the civic community desire to provide a moral and intellectual formation for their children. To prove that the contrarians have it wrong, all one has to do is to walk through any post-Vatican II Catholic elementary or secondary school to see that the grammar of Catholic schooling is not traditional, a cookbook of rigidly inflexible policies, procedures, rules, and recipes that place educators in Catholic schools into an ideological straight-jacket.

Because the grammar of Catholic schooling emerges from a living and vibrant religious tradition, educators in Catholic schools bear the responsibility of defining what the grammar implies, given their circumstances, concerning the educational program offered to their students. Further, the principle of subsidiarity (i.e., the making of these substantive educational decisions at the lowest level possible) ultimately recognizes the significance of teachers and administrators as well as their contributions to schooling, for subsidiarity empowers these courageous and selfless women and men to make those decisions that will translate the rules of the grammar of Catholic schooling into concrete educative experiences.

This grammar, then, is not static but dynamic, linking this generation's Catholic community with its forebears in previous generations. Fortunately, because this grammar represents the collective educational wisdom learned through centuries of experience, each new generation does not have to reinvent the educational wheel all over again. And, although the structure and organization of Catholic schooling (what I have called the syntax of Catholic schooling) may appear very different from generation to generation and from school to school, the underlying grammar is essentially the same.

Understanding the grammar of Catholic schooling clarifies just *why* Catholic schooling does *what* it does—or, accomplishes what it accomplishes—as the research studies examined in the previous chapter demonstrated these effects. As this grammar is the animating core of Catholic schooling, it provides a "purpose" or "mission" for Catholic schooling. It is a purpose that speaks to peoples' hearts and enables them to muster the courage it takes for parents and communities to make the sacrifices required to provide youth the very best moral and intellectual formation, one that emphasizes the development of each child's heart and mind (or, if you will, will and intellect).

For some parents and communities, courage might mean reordering priorities so they can afford the educational program their children truly need. For others, courage may mean devoting their lives and energies to educating youth, oftentimes at great personal sacrifice and cost. Yet, for some others, courage may require them to stand up and challenge the civic community, bringing to their consideration the failed, allegedly value-neutral, educational philosophy enshrined in the grammar of American public schooling. In sum, courage requires parents, pastors, bishops, educators, and students to discover the implicit meaning, the "why," that is found in the mundane requirements associated with Catholic schooling, the "what."

It is this final topic, what the grammar of Catholic schooling implies for U.S. Catholic educational leaders, to which we will now turn our attention.

Notes:

1. At a conference held at the University of Dayton (September 8-9, 1994), Bryk noted that rather than proclaim a compelling moral reason for Catholics to send their children to parochial schools, Baltimore III relied upon moral compulsion to require Catholic parents to send their children to parochial schools. In contrast, Bryk suggested that, if parents are to make the commitment required to send their children to Catholic schools, the post-Vatican II Church must proclaim a compelling moral reason to do so.

2. While any reasonable person would not contest that knowledge, skills, and social values are evident in any educated human being, it seems unreasonable to equate these means with true ends of education. Perhaps the ideas associated with 20th century psychometry reveal what Newman (1927), in a previous century, termed a "popular infidelity of the day," that is, an unprincipled ideology opposed to the truth but enjoying great popularity in the forum of public opinion. For Newman, public opinion is "the enemy of truth."

3. For a thorough analysis of this substantive case, see Jorgenson (1968).

4. Many believed that the "No Pass, No Play" measure had much to do with football, when it actually gored two prominent extra-curricular activities: the Future Farmers of America and the school band.

5. One problem this means-end technical rationality presented, however, is that it effectively reduced the dynamic concept of educating youth to a static concept, conveying instruction. It erroneously presumes that by improving educational technology, that is, curriculum and instruction, student learning surely would improve.

6. One of the most substantive developments for pedagogical practice has been the emergence of the "reflective practitioner" model. Advocated by Schön (1991), in particular, this model likens teaching to an artistic craft. It requires the practitioner to engage in open-ended conversation with herself, the materials she is working with, and others who possess the competence to help the practitioner to judge whether and to what degree she is accomplishing what she set out to accomplish. The reflective practitioner model is particularly useful for heightening teacher awareness of the moral dimensions of educating youth (Jacobs, 1995b).

Chapter 4

The grammar of Catholic schooling: What Catholic educational leaders do

Tyack and Tobin (1994) have asserted that during the 20th century American public schooling has generally remained impervious to change because there exists a transparent grammar governing the culture of American public schooling. While reformers have tinkered around the edges of public schooling, the operative rules of its grammar have allowed public schooling to remain resilient against the cyclical tides of reform. From the perspective of Catholic educational philosophy, this is truly a sad and most unfortunate state-of-affairs, if only because the grammar of public schooling has failed to equip youth with the moral experiences that inculcate the self-disciplines which make youth useful not only to themselves and society, but to religion as well.

Whether the topic concerns public or nonpublic schooling, one principle must not be overlooked: Education is about providing the most appropriate moral *and* intellectual formation for the nation's youth. If American public education is in trouble and stands in need of reform, one fact must be dealt with—the substance of American public schooling, its grammar, fails youth because it conveys little or no moral purpose for, or relationship to, human existence. When the moral purpose inherent in educating youth is lacking, symptoms indicating the presence of a deeper, dread disease gradually evince themselves. While one wave of reformers after another offers what appear to be sensible prescriptions to ameliorate the obvious maladies (that is, the symptoms of the disease), this incremental approach does little, if anything, to resolve the underlying issue (that is, the disease itself).

Currently, a fundamental lack of moral purpose evidences itself in the attitudes and beliefs of many educational leaders. These individuals include: parents, religious leaders, professional educators, and students.

A fundamental lack of moral purpose is evident in *parents* who care about educating their children but are not inspired to muster the courage or to devote the time it really takes to be actively involved in sustained efforts to see to it that their children receive the most appropriate moral and intellectual formation they deserve.

This lack of moral purpose manifests itself in *religious leaders* who pay lip service to pressing educational needs but fail to remind and to instruct their congregations about what God expects of His People. This failure is all the more grievous when these individuals feel no compunction after abdicating their educational leadership to a system of schooling that opposes the grammar of Catholic schooling.

This lack of moral purpose can be seen in those *superintendents and principals* who capably manage the educational bureaucracy so that schooling proceeds smoothly, but (oftentimes for political reasons) fail to articulate and enact their vision concerning what must be done to provide the fundamental moral and intellectual lessons youth need. This lack of courage suggests these educational leaders believe schools exist for educators rather than for students. The truth is otherwise.

Again, this lack of moral purpose evidences itself in *teachers* who know how to communicate curricular content but lack the enthusiasm, energy, and commitment to be educators who inspire their students to reach into and beyond the curriculum so that they might develop their physical, social, psychological, intellectual, and moral capital. Although these teachers may be comfortable with a rote, immediate approach to instructing youth, these teachers are not making authentic, deliberative decisions—the hallmark of a professional educator (Burlingame & Sergiovanni, 1993).

Finally, this lack of moral purpose is seen in *students* who simply attend school and jump aimlessly through the "hoops." Unfortunately, not only do these students experience little delight in attending school, but their dreams and aspirations are also disconnected from school. Their lack of moral purpose manifests itself as these students discover their fulfillment in the fleeting and transitory interests of the peer group or in the pleasures afforded by illegal substances. Or even worse, as they fail to value schooling, they drop-out of school altogether.

This sad litany of failure, identifying a fundamental collapse of educational leadership, stems primarily from a lack of purpose on the part of those citizens who should care very much about educating the nation's youth, if only because these young women and men are the nation's future. Perhaps, too, when other citizens contemplate the pervasive lack of educational leadership evidencing itself today, they are tempted to wonder, "Is there any hope?"

In contrast to the massive body of reform literature that castigates the ineffectiveness of public schooling and some of it even calling for a "reinvention of schooling" (Bush, 1991), research conducted during the past several decades has yielded an ample supply of data supporting the assertion that Catholic schooling has been particularly effective in conveying to youth the moral and intellectual purposes of schooling. Surprisingly, this depiction is particularly accurate especially for students from families providing lower levels of parental support and/or children from families with lower socioeconomic status, especially Blacks and Hispanics (Coleman & Hoffer, 1987; Greeley, 1982).

In light of the collapse of educational leadership, how accurate is this disconfirming evidence about Catholic schooling?

The simple fact is that, for Catholic schooling, a very different grammar informs educational practice. The grammar of Catholic schooling is comprised of six rules that represent the basic assumptions and values which bind the faith community as well as its parents, religious leaders, educators, and students in a purposeful project—the education of those youth who will provide the next generation's moral and intellectual leadership. *What* is done in Catholic schools today reflects a substantive purpose, *why* things are done. And, where these six rules permeate the school's functional means (namely, what is done in Catholic schools), moral and intellectual achievement has been demonstrated.[1] While many may find this outcome surprising, or somewhat puzzling, or perhaps even shocking, it really is not. Part of the reason has to do with "purpose," at least as organizational theorists have attempted to define and describe this phenomenon.

Educational purposing and Catholic schooling...

For generations, researchers have studied organizations and their leaders in an effort to develop an understanding about how the two interact, especially in successful organizations. Some researchers have theorized that when clear purposes characterize organizations, leaders and follows alike are motivated to contribute their human resources to the attainment of those purposes.

An early pioneer in the discipline of administrative science, Chester Barnard, was the first to stress the importance of clarity in organizational purpose if leaders are to effectively motivate others to desire and to devote themselves to achieving that purpose. As Barnard stated his case:

> ...an objective purpose that can serve as the basis for a cooperative system is one that is believed by the contributors (or potential contributors) to it to be the determined purpose of the organization. The inculcation of belief in the real existence of a common purpose is an essential executive function. (1938/1958, p. 87)

Although Barnard's focus on "executive functions" reflects an earlier era's attempt to express with greater precision the constituitive elements of leadership, Barnard did identify how important it is for leaders to inspire others to believe in and to be motivated by a shared vision concerning what ought to be the case. Barnard also theorized about how that desired state of affairs could be an organizational reality if every member of the organization were to share that common purpose.

Barnard's theory, it seems, is congruent with an observation asserted earlier, namely, that *what* people do in schools is important, but *why* people do what they do, the school's objective purpose, is what really motivates them to become engaged in and contribute their human

---

Define your school's primary purpose:
_____
_____
_____

List its major elements:
1)_____
2)_____
3)_____

resources to educating youth. For educational leaders, effectively communicating this purpose, the school's *raison d'être*, is perhaps the most essential educational leadership function. Constantly reiterating the school's purpose is incumbent upon all who are educational leaders, namely, parents, civic and religious leaders, professional educators, and students.

Twenty-nine years after Barnard first wrote about organizational purposes and their importance for both leaders and followers, Selznick (1957) asserted that the two essential leadership functions are: a) to define the institution's mission and role and b) to embody the institution's purpose. It is not enough, in Selznick's view, for leaders to proclaim an organizational mission or simply to reference it continuously as they interact with and represent their organization to various constituents. For educational leaders, Selznick implies that they not only need to motivate others to believe in and to share in the mission associated with schooling. In addition, educational leaders must also allow the mission of schooling to permeate the sinews of their being so that its purpose and meaning will be conveyed, as a seamless whole, through everything they do, whether in word or act.

When students, for example, experience their school's purpose being communicated by their teachers because these dedicated women and men truly believe in it and have faith that this purpose will make their students useful not only to themselves but also to their society and religion, students will then experience the motive to devote themselves more fully to their educational process, to take responsibility for their learning, and to link what they are doing today with their aspirations for tomorrow. In short, a clear educational purpose breeds intrinsic motivation.

Vaill (1984) expanded the theoretical foundation bequeathed by Barnard and Selznick when he proposed that effective leadership involves "purposing," that is, a "...continuous stream of actions by an organization's formal leadership which have the effect of inducing clarity consensus, and commitment regarding the organization's basic purposes" (p. 90). While purposing maintains fidelity to the expectations of those who chartered the organization in the first place by referencing these expectations, "[t]his does not mean that leaders merely preach conformity to these expectations" (p. 92). Instead, purposing might be likened to a journey (or, a search) by leaders and followers "for courses of action that are responsive to the ownership, substantively sound, not merely demagogic or exploitative, consistent with the system's evolving identity, and honest expressions of one's own values" (p. 93).

Educational purposing, Vaill would argue, requires those charged with responsibility for schooling youth to communicate effectively what schools exist for. If, for example, educational leaders are to engage in purposing, they cannot be content simply with encouraging teachers to adopt and adapt the latest educational trends and fads, purchasing the most modern instructional equipment, or cajoling tax-payers to construct ultra-modern, state-of-the-art facilities. All of these material entities are ancillary to schooling and have proven themselves to be of little or no significance, especially when a school and its programs lack substantive purpose.

Instead, purposing requires educational leaders who communicate convincingly why schooling has been, is, and will continue to be important to each student's life. Secondly, purposing requires educational leaders who convey clearly just how it is that what is being done in school today, even though it may be done somewhat differently given education's constantly changing context, does connect with and build upon what schools have been doing for generations. Thirdly, purposing requires educational leaders who express their values and devote themselves wholeheartedly to their subject, that is, their students. As Catholic schools have demonstrated clearly, even when schools and communities cannot afford ultra-modern, state-of-the-art equipment and facilities or to send teachers to expensive in-service or continuing education programs, purposing sets a framework that enables teachers to motivate youth to identify their needs with schooling.

Is it possible to see educational purposing in action? Vaill (1984) maintains it can, asserting that purposing evidences itself in three particular leadership behaviors.

First, purposing is evident when leaders spend extraordinary amounts of time making their organization work more effectively. "They put in many hours....The hours they put in are matters of frequent comment by those around them" (p. 94). Time is the "*when*" of leadership.

Where purposing is present, leaders also possess and manifest strong feelings about attaining the organization's purposes. Vaill states:

> [These leaders] care deeply about the system. This includes its purposes, its structure and conduct, its history, its future security and...they care about the people in the system. For the leader...constant energetic purposing is a natural expression of Feeling, i.e., of his or her own deep values and beliefs. Purposing is not a style or function which is adopted for some special occasion (p. 95).

Lastly, purposing manifests itself when a leader is focused—as the leader confronts the critical issues and variables threatening the organization's fundamental purpose. "[Leaders] know what few things are important, and in their statements and actions they make these priorities known....Focus is really Focus*ing* in dynamic terms: it is an ongoing process of choosing what to emphasize and what to leave alone" (pp. 96-97). In short, leaders do not get mired in administrivia. Focus is the "*what*" of leadership.

If educational leadership were likened to a drama (Starratt, 1993), what major themes would this three act drama convey?

1)_____
2)_____
3)_____

For Vaill, purposing is the when, the why, and the what of leadership. Purposing motivates people to dedicate extraordinary amounts of time, passionate feeling, and clear focus to the attainment of the organization's mission. For people with a purpose, work is not a job; it is an expression of and commitment to something they cherish and value.

Figure 4 summarizes Vaill's notion of organizational purposing and relates it to the work of Catholic educational leaders. In sum, more important than all of managerial concerns, human relations issues, and the myriad of thickets involved in providing instructional leadership—the resolution of which only provide evidence of a competently managed school (Sergiovanni, 1995), Vaill's theory would maintain that the substance of Catholic educational leadership is purposing. This leadership activity is what makes it possible for those involved in Catholic schooling to tap into the intrinsic motive for which they have freely chosen to participate in Catholic schooling and to dedicate themselves (that is, their time, their feeling, and their focus) to bring their school's mission to fulfillment.

Certainly, leaders who engage in purposing do think it is significant. But, what sets Catholic educational leaders who engage in purposing apart from other educational leaders and what enables their followers to bring the school's mission to fruition is how these leaders understand and act upon *why* they do *what* they do. Purposing explains just how it is that Catholic schools, and particularly inner-city Catholic high schools, are able to accomplish much more and with fewer resources when compared to other schools, particularly urban public schools.

Figure 4.

PURPOSING:

The Substance of Catholic Educational Leadership

For Catholic educational leaders, embodying the school's Catholic identity (i.e., its purpose) is the most substantive leadership activity:

- The inculcation of belief in the real existence of a common purpose is an essential executive function. (Barnard, 1958)
- The two essential functions of institutional leadership are:
  a) to define the institution's mission and role, and
  b) to embody the institution's purpose. (Selznick, 1957)
- Effective leadership involves "purposing," that is, a "...continuous stream of actions by an organization's formal leadership which have the effect of inducing clarity, consensus, and commitment regarding the organization's basic purposes." (Vaill, 1984)

Vaill's notion of purposing implies that the fundamental educational issue confronting Catholic educational leaders is not one of economics but leadership, that is, not finances but purposes. In light of this, Catholic schools need leaders who engage primarily in purposing not in managing their schools and fund-raising. Through purposing, Catholic educational leaders will challenge others to devote their time, their feeling, and their focus to this most important communal endeavor on behalf of youth.

Educational purposing and Catholic educational leadership...

Educational purposing has some very concrete implications for those who are concerned about the future of Catholic schooling.

For example, while many pastors make fervent appeals to their parishioners about the financial sacrifice needed if a parish is to sponsor a Catholic school, purposing suggests that appeals, no matter how fervent they may be, do not inspire the courage it takes for the parish community to muster its time, feeling, and focus to provide the most appropriate moral and intellectual formation for its youth. Furthermore, soliciting a second collection for the parish school on the first Sunday of each month may help a pastor stem the tide of some bill collectors, but a second collection fails to convey to parishioners how their act of generosity represents a personal commitment to the parish's youth and the future of the Church itself.

Then, too, when diocesan schools offices post advertisements on billboards identifying how many dollars a particular Catholic school saves taxpayers, the sign may cause a passerby to wonder how it is possible for that school to save the state so much money. However, purposing reminds diocesan schools offices that these advertisements are ineffective for, ultimately, they fail to communicate why it is in the larger community's best interest that every student receive an education shaped according to the grammar of Catholic schooling.

Educational purposing on behalf of Catholic schooling occurs when parents, bishops, vicars for education, superintendents, pastors, educators, and students inculcate belief in what the most appropriate educational program really is, transform doubts into a vibrant reality, and embody that purpose in their lives by continuously reinterpreting what transpires in Catholic schools and by referencing the school's fundamental purposes—as these have been conveyed through the heritage of Catholic schooling—in all that they do. In short, Catholic educational leadership is embodied not only in individuals but more importantly in the search that the entire Catholic community undertakes to translate Scripture and Tradition, to interpret the Church's educational heritage and policies, and to muster all of the human, fiscal, and educational resources it has into an educational program that will provide for the moral and intellectual needs of its youth. As Baltimore III correctly pointed out more than one century ago, every Catholic child deserves this formation and parishes should consider themselves deficient until that want is supplied (Nolan, 1984).

To supply for this need, the grammar of Catholic schooling implies several things. First, it implies that Catholic educational leaders must be more than conversant with and understanding of the fundamental rules associated with this grammatical system. Words and ideas are powerful but, in as far as listeners are concerned, only when these words and ideas are applied to the educational context within which educational leaders exercise their responsibilities. A second implication, stemming from the first, is that if Catholic educational leaders are to inspire others to know, understand, and apply the grammar of Catholic schooling, they must proclaim the six fundamental principles, or rules governing Catholic schooling. They do this in the most compelling way by dedicating vast amounts of personal time, intense feeling, and clarity of focus to further the teleological ends of Catholic schooling, viz., the salvation of their students' souls through a program of moral and intellectual formation.

For Catholic educational leaders, Vaill's (1984) research implies that when U.S. Catholic educational leaders know and understand the grammar of Catholic schooling and when they proclaim the purpose of Catholic schooling through their words and actions, their followers will become intrinsically motivated to contribute their time, feeling, and focus to achieve those purposes. For example, *Parents* will be challenged to fulfill their divine obligation to provide the very best moral and intellectual educational formation for their children. Parents will dedicate their time, feeling, and focus to seek out and, if necessary, to challenge both the Church (to assist them in their efforts to provide a sound program of moral training) and the state (to aid them in providing the best possible intellectual training) for their children.

Bishops will devote their time, feeling, and focus to proclaim to those entrusted to their ministry why Catholic schools do what they do, why this is of particular importance to the U.S. Catholic Church, as well has how this alternate to public education is of paramount value to the national interest. These Catholic educational leaders will also challenge any unprincipled educational ideology that does not promote the most appropriate educational program for youth.

Vicars for education and *diocesan superintendents* will be motivated to devote their time, feeling, and focus to translate this important message into workable educational policies that can be used to frame decision-making in local schools. These Catholic educational leaders will endeavor to assist parents and educators to clarify what Catholic schooling truly is and will be for their children.

Pastors and *educators in Catholic schools* will dedicate their time, feeling, and focus to respond to the educational needs of youth. These Catholic educational leaders will engage in heady and, yes, sometimes very heated conversation concerning what they must do as a community to develop those young women and men who will be the next generation's Catholic educational leaders.

Students, too, will be challenged to devote their time, feeling, and focus to develop their hearts and minds so that they will be capable of functioning one day as effective national leaders. More importantly, students will be challenged to devote their time, feeling, and focus to develop their power of will so that they will be prepared not only to accept but also to exercise their leadership role as citizens of God's Kingdom.

If the reformers are accurate in their assessment that American public education is ineffective, what public education manifests today is a direct consequence of the application of the grammar of public schooling. Particularly in those schools where youth fail not only to learn the important knowledge, skills, and values associated with citizenship in a modern, pluralistic democracy, but more importantly, where they fail to practice and exercise the rights and responsibilities associated with adult citizenship, these symptoms betray a much deeper disease, a loss of purpose.

Sadly, in those neighborhoods, towns, and cities where public schools have been judged to be derelict in their mission to educate American youth, it has become convenient to point the finger-of-blame in every direction rather than squarely at the failed grammar of public schooling. The fact is that educational leaders have failed to communicate the purposes of public schooling, at least in so far as these purposes are not conveyed in those schools where students fail to master the basic knowledge and skills required of adult citizens, where students engage in illegal and illicit behaviors to avoid school, and where truancy and drop-out rates near 50 per cent.

To invoke Newman's analogy, the grammar of Catholic schooling provides those who study and use it an ideal standard of what is admirable and what is absurd, a certain habit of mind that helps them to evaluate schooling accurately, precisely, or as Newman would have it, truly. It should not prove surprising, then, that Catholic schools are successful when compared to their counterparts in the public sector, if only for the reason that U.S. Catholic educational leaders have provided youth the most appropriate educational program. They have communicated the purposes of Catholic schooling and, in turn, this has motivated students to learn the basic knowledge, skills, and values required of adult citizens, to engage in more wholesome behavior, and to stay in and graduate from school. And, almost surprisingly (but not so to those who understand how leadership and purposing motivate high performance), all of this has come at a lower per student cost.

Looking toward the 21st century, it has been suggested that the human race is quickly leaving the Industrial Age behind and is speeding head-first into a new Information Age. If these sages and pundits are correct, humanity will soon discover itself in the midst of a post-modern, post-industrial world where few touchstones exist to aid humanity in making important decisions about how best to prepare youth for a very obscure future. One thing does seem certain, however. Education will continue to be critical to that future.

In the face of these challenges and the resilience of the grammar of public schooling against the tides of educational reform, the U.S. Catholic community will need more than ever to exercise leadership by engaging in educational purposing. Its words and actions must convey the heartfelt conviction that God is the beginning and end of human existence, that education is essentially a moral endeavor, that parents bear primary responsibility for the education of their children, that the subject of education is the student, that teaching is an intimate communication between souls, and that educational decisions are best made locally. Furthermore, as the U.S. Catholic community engages in educational purposing, they will need to devote increased amounts of time to developing concrete resolutions to pesky educational issues, to become more focused concerning what is truly necessary for youth, and to communicate genuine passion for the moral and intellectual formation of youth. Otherwise, their co-religionists and fellow citizens will be neither inspired nor motivated to contribute their time, feeling, and focus to this penultimate endeavor.

It must be recognized, however, that while the grammar of Catholic schooling provides a standard defining what educational programs for youth must include, the grammar of Catholic schooling is silent when it comes to resolving particularly nettlesome issues. The grammar leaves it up to Catholic educational leaders to be creative in applying its rules to the concrete educational realities at hand. The grammar of Catholic schooling, then, places parents, bishops, pastors, principals and teachers, and students in the position of having to exercise educational leadership and to bear moral responsibility for the decisions they make.

It will be today's Catholic educational leaders, those who accept these challenges and who endeavor to resolve the educational issues confronting the U.S. Catholic community today, who will have fulfilled their vocation to proclaim the Gospel to all peoples (Mark 16:15). It will be these disciples, like their forebears at Baltimore III, who will have insured that the Gospel will be faithfully proclaimed not only to the next generation but well into the new millennium.

Notes:

1. Even more impressive and significant, I believe, is that schools which attend to the moral fiber of education do not exhibit decreased student achievement. When the moral fiber of education is attended to, as it is in Catholic schooling, parents tend to be more involved, teachers tend to expand the curricular limits as they struggle to become educators (and with fewer resources), and students tend to value what they are learning even if they do not experience it as all that terribly exciting.

References

Ackerman, R. H., Donaldson, G. A., & van der Bogert, R. (1996). *Making sense as a school leader: Persisting questions, creative opportunities*. San Francisco, CA: Jossey-Bass.

Alexander, K. L. (1987). Cross-sectional comparisons of public and private school effectiveness: A review of evidence and issues. In E. H. Haertel, T. James & H. M. Levin (Eds.), *Comparing public & private schools* (Vol. 2: School achievement). New York: Falmer Press.

Alexander, K. L., & Pallas, A. M. (1983). Private schools and public policy: New evidence on cognitive achievement. *Sociology of Education, 56*, 170-182.

Aronowitz, S., & Giroux, H. A. (1991). *Postmodern education: Politics, culture, and social criticism*. Minneapolis, MN: University of Minnesota Press.

Arons, S. (1976, February). The separation of school and state: *Pierce* revisited. *Harvard Educational Review, 46*(1), 76-104.

ASCD *Education Update*. (1997, March). Proposed position: Parents' rights. *Education Update, 39*(2), 4.

Augustine of Hippo. (1992). *Confessions* (F. J. Sheed, Trans.). Indianapolis, IN: Hackett Publishing Company, Inc.

Augustine of Hippo. (1949). *The greatness of the soul & the teacher* (J. M. Colleran, Trans.). New York, NY: Newman Press.

Barnard, C. (1938/1958). *The functions of the executive*. Boston: Harvard University Press.

Beck, L. G., & Murphy, J. (1992). Searching for a robust understanding of the principalship. *Educational Administration Quarterly, 28*(3), 387-396.

Bryk, A. S., Lee, V. E., & Holland, P. B. (1993). *Catholic schools and the common good*. Cambridge, MA: Harvard University Press.

Burlingame, M., & Sergiovanni, T. (1993). Some questions about school leadership and communication theory. *Journal of Management Systems, 5*(2), 51-61.

Bush, G. (1991). Appendix II "Remarks by the President announcing America 2000, The White House, April 18, 1991." In U.S. Department of Education, *America 2000 an education strategy*. Washington, DC: U.S. Department of Education.

Callahan, R. E. (1962). *Education and the cult of efficiency: A study of the social forces that have shaped the administration of the public schools*. Chicago: University of Chicago Press.

Carnegie Council on Adolescent Development. (1989). *Turning points: Preparing American youth for the 21st century*. New York: Carnegie Corporation.

Carr, D. (1991). *Educating the virtues*. New York: Routledge.

Coleman, J. S. (1987a). Families and schools. *Educational Researcher, 6*, 32-38.

Coleman, J. S. (1987b). Social capital and the development of youth. *Momentum, 18*(19), 6-8.

Coleman, J. S. (1988). Social capital and the creation of human capital. *American Sociologist, 94*, 5095-5120.

Coleman, J. S. (1991). *Parental involvement in education.* Washington, DC: U.S. Department of Education.

Coleman, J., Hoffer, T., & Kilgore, S. (1982). *High school achievement: Public, Catholic and private schools compared.* New York: Basic Books.

Coleman, J., & Hoffer, T. (1987). *Public and private high schools: The impact of communities.* New York: Basic Books.

Convey, J. (1992). *Catholic schools make a difference: Twenty-five years of research.* Washington, DC: National Catholic Educational Association.

Cutler, W. W. (1989). Cathedral of culture: The schoolhouse in American educational thought and practice since 1820. *History of Education Quarterly, 29*(1), 1-40.

Deal, T. E., & Peterson, K. D. (1990). *The principal's role in shaping school culture.* Washington, DC: U.S. Department of Education, Office of Educational Research and Improvement.

Dewey, J. (1916/1944). *Democracy and education: An introduction to the philosophy of education.* New York: The Free Press.

Dolan, J. P. (1985). *The American Catholic experience.* New York: Image Books.

D'Souza, D. (1991). *Illiberal education: The politics of race and sex on campus.* New York: Free Press.

Educational Leadership. (1993). Character education (special issue). *51*(3), November.

Educational Leadership. (1993). Can public schools accommodate Christian fundamentalists? (special issue). *51*(4), December-January.

Eisner, E. (1985). *The educational imagination* (2nd ed.). New York: Macmillan.

Etzioni, A. (1993). *The spirit of community: Rights, responsibilities, and the Communitarian agenda.* New York: Crown Publishers, Inc.

Foster, W. P. (1980a). The changing administrator: Developing managerial praxis. *Eductional Theory, 30*(1), 11-23.

Foster, W. P. (1980b). Administration and the crisis in legitimacy: A review of Habermasian thought. *Harvard Educational Review, 50*(4), 496-505.

Getzels, J. W., & Guba, E. G. (1957). Social behavior and the administrative process. *The School Review, 29*, 30-40.

Goldberger, A.S., & Cain, G. G. (1982). The causal analysis of cognitive outcomes in the Coleman, Hoffer and Kilgore report. *Sociology of Education, 55*, 103-122.

Greeley, A. M. (1982). *Catholic high schools and minority students*. New Brunswick, NJ: Transaction Books.

Greeley, A. M. (1989, November). My research on Catholic schools. *Chicago Studies, 28*(3), 245-263.

Greeley, A. M., & Rossi, P. H. (1966). *The education of Catholic Americans*. Chicago, IL: Aldine Press.

Griffiths, D. E. (1988). Administrative theory. In N. Boyan (Ed.), *Handbook of research on educational administration* (pp. 27-51). New York: Longman.

Hancock, L., & Kalb, C. (1996, June 24). Education—A room of their own: Public schools try single-sex classes. *Newsweek*, 127(26), 76.

Hansen, L. S., Hansen, S., Walker, J., & Flom, B. (1995). *Growing smart: What's working for girls in school*. Washington, DC: Educational Foundation of the American Association University Women.

Harvard Educational Review. (1981, Nov.). Special issue.

Heynes, B., & Hilton, T. L. (1982). The cognitive tests for High School and Beyond: An assessment. *Sociology of Education, 55*, 89-192.

Hirsch, E.J. (1987). *Cultural Literacy: What Every American Needs to Know*. Boston: Houghton Mifflin.

Jackall, R. (1988). *Moral mazes*. New York: Oxford University Press.

Jacobs, R. M. (1995a). *The 12th annual Seton-Neumann lecture: The grammar of Catholic schooling*. Washington, DC: United States Catholic Conference.

Jacobs, R. M. (1995b). Communicating about Teaching: Pre-service teacher curricula and communication theory. In J. Murphy & M. O'Hair (Eds.), *Yearbook of the Association of Teacher Educators* (pp. 163-186). Newbury Park, CA: Sage Publications.

Jacobs, R. M. (1996). *The vocation of the Catholic Educator: Reflections for Catholic teachers and administrators*. Washington, DC: National Catholic Education Association.

Jacobs, R. M. (1997a/April 2). *The ethical basis of Catholic educational leadership: The authority of the Catholic school principal*. Paper delivered at the National Catholic Educational Association Annual Convention, Minneapolis, MN.

Jacobs, R. M. (1997b/May 30). The future belongs to those who control the schools: Catholic schools and the religious who taught in them. Paper delivered at the Lilly Foundation/Catholic University of America symposium, *American Legacy at the Crossroads: Research Synthesis and Policy Analysis of Catholic Schools*, Washington, DC.

John Paul II. (1991). *Centesimus annus: Encyclical letter of the supreme pontiff John Paul II on the one hundredth anniversary of Rerum novarum.* Rome, Italy: n.p.

Johnson, G. (1942). Our task in the present crisis. NCEA *Bulletin, 38,* 63-72.

Jorgenson, L. P. (1968). The Oregon school law of 1922: Passage and sequel. *Catholic Historical Review, 54,* 455-66.

Keith, T. Z., & Page, E. B. (1985). Do Catholic schools improve minority student achievement? *American Educational Research Journal, 22,* 337-349.

Kohn, A. (1997, February). How not to teach values: A critical look at character education. *Phi Delta Kappan, 78*(6),429-439.

Lannie, V. P., & Diethorn, B. C. (1968, Spring). For the honor and glory of God: The Philadelphia bible riots of 1840. *History of Education Quarterly, 8,* 44-106.

LaPlante, R. L. (1992). The Catholic school: A community with a changing language. In C. DiGiovanni (Ed.), *The philosophy of Catholic education* (pp. 31-56). Ottawa, Ontario, Canada: Novalis.

Lasley, T. J. (1997, April). The missing ingredient in character education. *Phi Delta Kappan, 78*(8), 654-655.

Leo XIII. (1887/1979). Common duties and interests. In The Benedictine Monks of Solesemes, *Education: Papal teachings* (A. Robeschini, Trans., pp. 104-108). Boston, MA: St. Paul Editions.

Lickona, T. (1991). *Educating for character: How our schools can teach respect and responsibility.* New York: Bantam Books.

Lieberman, A., & Miller, L. (1984). *Teachers, their work and their world.* Arlington, VA: Association for Supervision and Curriculum Development.

Lightfoot, S. L. (1983). *The good high school: Portraits of character and culture.* New York: Basic Books, Inc.

Lortie, D. (1975). *School teacher.* Chicago, IL: University of Chicago Press.

Luke, A. (1991). The secular word: Catholic reconstructions of Dick and Jane. In M. W. Apple & L. K. Christian-Smith, *The politics of the textbook* (pp. 166-190). New York: Routledge.

Maritain, J. (1943). *Education at the crossroads.* New Haven, CN: Yale University Press.

McCarren, E. P. (1966). *The origin and early years of the National Catholic Educational Association.* Unpublished dissertation, Catholic University of America, Washington, DC.

McKechnie, J. L. (Ed.). (1983). *Webster's new twentieth century dictionary* (2nd ed.). New York: Simon and Schuster.

McLaren, P. (1986). Making Catholics: The ritual production of conformity in a Catholic junior high school. *Journal of Education, 168*(2), 55-77.

McPartland, J. M., & McDill, E. L. (1982). Control and differentiation in the structure of American education. *Sociology of Education, 55*, 77-88.

Murnane, R. J. (1981). Evidence, analysis, and unanswered questions. *Harvard Educational Review, 51*, 483-489.

Murphy, J. (1992). *The landscape of leadership preparation: Reframing the education of school administrators.* Newbury Park, CA: Corwin Press, Inc.

Murphy, J. (1993). Alternative designs, new directions. In J. Murphy (Ed.), *Preparing tomorrow's school leaders: Alternative designs.* University Park, PA: UCEA.

National Catholic Educational Association. (1986). *1986 data bank historical data.* Washington, DC: National Catholic Educational Association.

National Catholic Educational Association. (1988). *Visions and Values in the Catholic School.* Washington, DC: National Catholic Educational Association.

National Catholic Educational Association. (1996). *United States Catholic elementary and secondary schools 1995-96: The annual statistical report on schools, enrollment and staffing.* Washington, DC: National Catholic Educational Association.

National Commission on Excellence in Education. (1983). *A nation at risk: The imperative for educational reform.* Washington, DC: U.S. Government Printing Office.

National Conference of Catholic Bishops. (1986). *Economic justice for all.* Washington, DC: NCCB/USCC.

Neuhaus, R. J. (1987). *The Catholic moment.* San Francisco: Harper & Row.

Newman, J. H. (1927/1987). *The idea of a university defined and illustrated.* Chicago: Loyola University Press.

Noell, J. (1982). Public and Catholic schools: A reanalysis of "Public and Private Schools." *Sociology of Education, 55*, 123-132.

Noell, J. (1983). A response to Coleman, Hoffer and Kilgore. *Sociology of Education, 56*, 203.

Nolan, H. J. (Ed.). (1984). Pastoral letter issued by the third plenary Council of Baltimore. In *Pastoral letters of the United States Catholic bishops* (pp. 209-240). Washington, DC: National Catholic Conference of Bishops/United States Catholic Conference.

Pelikan, J. (1971). *The Christian tradition: A history of the development of doctrine* (Vol. 1). Chicago: University of Chicago Press.

Pierce v. Society of Sisters, 268 U.S. 510 (1925).

Pius XI. (1929/1979). Education of the redeemed man. In The Benedictine Monks of Solesemes, *Education: Papal teachings* (A. Robeschini, Trans., pp. 200-248). Boston, MA: St. Paul Editions.

Pius XI. (1931). *Quadragesimo anno: Encyclical letter of the Supreme Pontiff Pius XI on the fortieth anniversary of Rerum Novarum.* Rome: n.p.

Pius XII. (1945/1979). The vocation of the teacher. In The Benedictine Monks of Solesemes, *Education: Papa teachings* (A. Robeschini, Trans., pp. 336-345). Boston, MA: St. Paul Editions.

Pius XII. (1949/1979). The idea of complete Christian education. In The Benedictine Monks of Solesemes, *Education: Papal teachings* (A. Robeschini, Trans., pp. 367-371). Boston, MA: St. Paul Editions.

Pius XII. (1954a/1979). The condition of the Christian teacher. In The Benedictine Monks of Solesemes, *Education: Papal teachings* (A. Robeschini, Trans., pp. 476-481). Boston, MA: St. Paul Editions.

Pius XII. (1954b/1979). Good teachers. In The Benedictine Monks of Solesemes, *Education: Papal teachings* (A. Robeschini, Trans., pp. 482-85). Boston, MA: St. Paul Editions.

Pius XII. (1955/1979). The Catholic teacher. In The Benedictine Monks of Solesemes, *Education: Papal teachings* (A. Robeschini, Trans., pp. 512-21). Boston, MA: St. Paul Editions.

Plato. (1992). *The republic* (G. M. A. Grube, Trans.). Indianapolis, IN: Hackett Publishing Company.

Powell, A. G., Farrar, E., & Cohen, D. K. (1985). *The shopping mall high school: Winners and losers in the educational marketplace.* Boston, MA: Houghton Mifflin.

Prestine, N. A., & Thurston, P. W. (Eds.). (1994). New directions in educational administration: Policy, preparation, and practice. *Advances in educational administration* (Volume 3). Greenwich, CN: JAI Press Inc.

Quade, Q. (1996). *Financing education: The struggle between governmental monopoly and parental control.* New Brunswick, NJ: Transaction Publishers.

Raudenbush, S., & Bryk, A. (1986). A hierarchical model for studying school effects. *Sociology of Education, 59,* 1-17.

Ravitch, D. (1994, May 27). *Somebody's children: Expanding educational opportunity for all American children.* An unpublished manuscript prepared for a conference at Princeton University.

Sarason, S. B. (1995). *Parental involvement and the political principle: Why the existing governance structure of schools should be abolished.* San Francisco: Jossey-Bass.

Schein, E. (1984). Coming to a new awareness of organizational culture. *Sloan Management Review, 25*(2), 3-15.

Schön, D. A. (1991). *Educating the reflective practitioner.* San Francisco: Jossey-Bass.

Selznick, P. (1957). *Leadership in administration*. New York: Harper & Row.

Sergiovanni, T. J. (1995). *The principalship: A reflective-practice perspective* (3rd ed.). Needham, MA: Allyn and Bacon.

Sergiovanni, T. J., & Starratt, R. J. (1988). *Supervision: Human perspectives* (4th ed.). New York: McGraw-Hill.

Shahan, T. J. (1917). Address. *CEA Bulletin, 4*(14), 42-45.

Smylie, M. A. (1992) Teacher participation in school decision making: Assessing willingness to participate. *Educational Evaluation and Policy Analysis, 14*(1), 53-67.

Sociology of Education 55 (April/July, 1982), *56* (October, 1983); *58* (July, 1985). Special issues.

Sommerfeld, M. (1994, August 3) Study compares religious education of parish programs, Catholic schools. *Education Week, 13*, 13.

Starratt, R. J. (1993). *The drama of leadership*. Bristol, PA: The Falmer Press.

Starratt, R. J. (1994). *Building an ethical school: A practical response to the moral crisis in schools*. Bristol, PA: The Falmer Press.

Tönnies, F. (1964). *Community & society (Gemeinschaft und Gesellschaft*, 2nd ed., C. P. Loomis, Trans., Ed.). East Lansing, MI: The Michigan State University Press.

Tyack, D., & Tobin, W. (1994). The "grammar" of schooling: Why has it been so hard to change? *American Educational Research Journal, 31*(3), 452-479.

Vaill, P. B. (1986). The purposing of high-performing systems. In T. J. Sergiovanni & J. E. Corbally (Eds.), *Leadership and organizational culture* (pp. 89-104). Urbana, IL: University of Illinois Press.

Viteritti, J. P. (1996, Summer). Stacking the deck for the poor. *The Brookings Review, 14*(3), 10-13.

Walch, T. (1996). *Parish school: American Catholic parochial education from colonial times to the present*. New York: Crossroad Herder.

Weber, M. (1930/1992). *The Protestant ethic and the spirit of capitalism* (A. Giddens, Trans.). New York: Routledge.

Weick, K. E. (1982). Administering education in loosely coupled schools. *Phi Delta Kappan, 63*(10), 673-76.

Willms, J. D. (1984). School effectiveness within the public and private sectors: An evaluation. *Evaluation Review, 8*, 113-135.

Willms, J. D. (1985). Catholic-school effects on academic achievement: New evidence from the High School and Beyond Follow-Up Study. *Sociology of Education, 58*, 98-114.

Willms, J. D. (1987). Patterns of academic achievement in public and private schools: Implications for public policy and future research. In E. H. Haertel, T. James & H. M. Levin (Eds.),

Comparing public & private schools (Vol. 2: School achievement). New York: Falmer Press.

Yeager, R. J., Benson, P. L., Guerra, M. J., & Manno, B. V. (1985). *The Catholic high school: A national portrait*. Washington, DC: National Catholic Educational Association.

Yob, I. M. (1994, November). Reflections on an experimental course: Religion and the public schools. *Phi Delta Kappan, 76*(3), 234-238.